COMPLETE GUIDE

TO SELLING INTANGIBLES

COMPLETE GUIDE

TO SELLING INTANGIBLES

Abbott P. Smith

Parker Publishing Company, Inc.
West Nyack, New York

© 1971 BY

PARKER PUBLISHING COMPANY, INC.
WEST NYACK, NEW YORK

LIBRARY OF CONGRESS
CATALOG CARD NUMBER: 75-150092

PRINTED IN THE UNITED STATES OF AMERICA
ISBN-0-13-160374-4
B&P

WHAT YOU WILL FIND IN THIS BOOK

As an intangibles salesman, whether in the expanding universe of service sales or in the world of intangibles "products" such as Mutual Funds, Stocks, Bonds and Insurance, you need no complicated plans, no massive investment of capital or time to increase your earnings. To start your sales curve climbing, you need only apply *consistently* the skills and techniques outlined and detailed in this book.

The secret to success in intangibles selling, and the key to the methods illustrated in this book, lies in a customer-oriented, problem-solving state of mind. From my own experience and from the many firing line cases I have collected over many years in the field, I have compressed this selling state of mind into three major parts:

1. *Be your prospect's representative.* Walk into every interview with the thought that you are there to help the prospect buy something that will satisfy *his* needs and solve *his* problems. This attitude will shine through your presentation—helping you gain a long-standing client rather than a one-shot sale.

2. *Put your prospect's interests in the center of your presentation.* When you ask about and discuss his needs *before* you start to sell, you demonstrate in action your conviction that you represent his interests as well as your own.

3. *Have a constructive reason for every customer contact.* It can be large: the solution to a personal or business problem. It can be small: an item of information. But when you are *always* prepared to be helpful in some way—large or small—with every client contact, your sales-to-calls ratio will inevitably start climbing.

Each of these points will be elaborated upon throughout this Guide. Also this Guide focuses solidly on the need to sell yourself in such a way that you establish confidence, are always welcome and keep your customers buying. Success in intangibles selling rests largely on frequent customer contact and continued repeat sales; unlike the man selling a hard product, the intangibles salesman often deals primarily with more or less elusive ideas.

But certainly the constructive salesman does not shy away from asking for the order. Rather he builds up to it in problem-solving fashion. As he might put it: "I sell because I walk in with the thought that I will never sell the prospect anything unless I am sure it will have meaning and value for him." Analysis of thousands of cases, in large firms and small, demonstrates beyond all dispute that the *constructive* problem-solving customer-oriented salesman almost always gains a decided competitive advantage. And my own experiences as salesman, sales consultant and trainer confirms it.

The very week I was writing this Introduction I made a sale which throws a dramatic highlight on my central theme. I received a call from a man I hadn't done business with for eight years. "Abbott," he said, "I'm calling you now because you're the only insurance man I've known who hasn't tried to load me with more than I needed at any one time. I've just started a new business and it will take three or four years before I know if it will pan out. Meanwhile, I want to insure my five associates for a total of $1,000,000. I'll leave the details to you." As you can imagine, I almost toppled off my chair when I heard that. But I managed to stammer my thanks and assure him that I'd work out a plan immediately. Since I could write my own ticket, I might easily have earned a nice fat commission with a nice fat plan. However, because the business might fold in three or four years, I felt the safest bet would be term insurance which could be converted to regular life if the business proved sound.

Two days after the call I was in my client's office writing out a million dollar's worth of policies. The client was pleased that I hadn't tried to oversell him. And if the business eventually converted to ordinary life, I'll be the fair-haired boy again—this time, with $38,000 in commissions on tap. What if the business flops? My client will still be one man I can always count on for prospect referrals. That's the gilt-edged bonus the constructive salesman usually finds at the end of the rainbow.

Abbott Smith

ACKNOWLEDGMENTS

Next to the thrill of *finishing* a project like a book comes the pleasure of writing the Acknowledgments. Here I can try thank all the people who have, willingly or unwillingly, knowingly or unknowingly, helped me write the book! After more than thirty years of selling and teaching others how, it's impossible to single out everyone who has provided ideas which have been used in or adapted to my own salesmanship. Many I have used in sales training programs for client companies. Often someone else's idea has helped me make an important sale and I no longer can remember or find that person to say a heartfelt "Thank you!" I hope the *Complete Guide to Selling Intangibles* will be looked upon in some measure as my sincerest thanks to all of them.

One man in particular has been especially helpful in writing this book. I want to thank Dr. Arthur Mitchell, my principal associate in ASA Training Consultants, Inc., for his help in planning and organizing the material, for contributing many original ideas, and for assuming heavy editorial responsibility.

Others to whom I am grateful for particular ideas and encouragement are William J. Driscoll, Managing Director, Sales & Marketing Executives—International; J. Norton Dunn, Director, Business Education, Dun & Bradstreet and Chairman of the Sales Training Division of the American Society for Training & Development; Kenneth O. Michel, Programs Manager, Executive Education Operations, General Electric Company; Robert Whyte, Director, Development & Training, Hornblower & Weeks, Hemphill Noyes; Porter Henry, President, Porter Henry & Company; and Richard Stern, President, Richard Stern Associates.

My thanks, too, to all the others, named and unnamed, whose successful selling ideas will be found in this book. May they help the reader as much as they have helped me.

CONTENTS

Part IV
KEEPING YOUR INTANGIBLES CUSTOMERS SOLD

COMPLETE GUIDE

TO SELLING INTANGIBLES

PART I

Managing Your Territory
in Intangibles Selling

1

How to Prospect Constructively
for More Intangibles Sales

"What is the best asset a salesman can have?"

When *Sales Management* posed that question to its knowledgeable readers, more than 75% replied: "A well-kept, up-to-date prospect file."

And the general sales manager of a leading insurance company added categorically: "I have yet to see a man succeed in selling who doesn't know how to prospect. Many salesmen concentrate on the 'bread and butter' sales to their established customers, leaving little time for prospecting. Sooner or later, they're in trouble."

Every Sale Is a Case for Prospecting

Most of us who sell intangibles will agree with these sentiments. The trouble is, we don't always follow through on the implications.

You know how it is. You've just made an important sale. So you luxuriate a little in the feeling of a job well done. Maybe you even start figuring how you'll spend your commission.

Celebrating is fine—provided you also start thinking about replenishing your prospect file. *For the man you just sold is no longer a prospect.*

"But he's a customer, now," you may well retort. "And if I've heard it once, I've heard it a hundred times: 'Customers are your best prospects.' So why the fuss?"

Take a Look at the Figures

That's true enough. The second sale to a buyer is easier than the first: and probably more profitable too.

But the figures tell another—and sadder—story. For old customers die or fade away; to the tune of about 20% a year. You've got to replace them if you want to stay alive as a salesman.

And that's not the half of it. To take another fairly average figure—though this varies somewhat from field to field and salesman to salesman—you've got to call on ten prospects to land one new customer.

That means you've got to find 200 new prospects for every 20 customers you lose. Like the Red Queen in *Alice,* you've got a powerful lot of running to do just to stay in the same place.

A Program Will Dc It

Now don't let it get you down, for a well-conceived prospecting routine will keep you on top of the situation, conserve your energy, save your time, and increase your earnings.

The basics of a sound prospecting program break down into four main areas.
1. Develop a plan.
2. Build and maintain a prospecting inventory.
3. Qualify your prospects.
4. Work your list to best advantage.

1. DEVELOP A PLAN

The successful salesman never stops prospecting. He knows he cannot safely ignore any lead from any source if he is to maintain his income.

But to conserve his selling time, he prospects by plan.

Objectives Come First

As a salesman, you are an independent businessman. Prospects are your "inventory"; you must check out and replenish your list as carefully as a dealer checks his stock. And you'll do a better job of replacing "inventory" when you know exactly what you're shooting for, every day, every week, every month.

Most good salesmen know how many prospects they must hit to make a single sale. And they know how many sales they need to make the kind of living they want.

Figure this out for your own selling circumstances, and you'll soon know how many prospects you must add to your "stock" in a given period of time. If you require 40 good prospects a month, then aim for at least two new prospects every working day. And aim to replace every prospect you cross off your list as a dud.

Do Some Prospecting Every Day

To achieve your objectives, make prospecting a daily practice. When planning your sales calls for the day, allow time for prospecting in the same vicinity.

Plan For the Doldrums

Most of us hit days when we just don't feel like selling. Instead of letting the day go completely to waste, get out and do some prospecting.

Often, this will pay an added dividend, for the productive effort you put into prospecting may snap you out of the doldrums, may put you in a frame of mind to reach out for sales.

You've drawn up your objectives and you're looking for prospects. But where do you do your looking? That takes us to the second part of your prospecting program.

2. HOW TO BUILD AND MAINTAIN A PROSPECTING INVENTORY

Every company will help its salesmen build their prospecting lists. And that's all to the good. But the man who is going places is the one who actively builds his own.

You can build up your prospect file from published sources: chamber of commerce lists; business and professional directories; property owner lists; trade and professional journals; and the like:

Such lists have two inherent weaknesses: they are impersonal, and they cannot pinpoint those most likely to need your services. In any case, all they require is the time and effort necessary to transfer the names to your files.

Personalized Referrals

Far more meaningful are personalized referrals; names suggested by people who know and may influence them. There are many techniques for harvesting a plentiful crop of choice referrals. In this section, concentrate on the five which have proven particularly effective in the intangible sales field.

FIVE PROSPECTING TECHNIQUES

Some salesmen apply all of them—choosing the method most appropriate to a given situation. Others, by trial and error, settle upon those most suitable to their ways of working. Common sense and experimentation will dictate the best techniques for you.

1. The "Pebble-in-the-Pool" Technique

Did you ever drop a pebble in a quiet pool of water? After the first splash, ripples spread out in perfect circles from the point where the pebble lands. As these ripples spread, they soon cover the whole pool—then reach into all the little nooks and crannies at the edges.

That's how it is in selling. The first personalized referrals dropped into a prospecting pool start a rippling effect that radiates to the outermost edges of your marketing area. An example will show how this works.

Step 1. Pick a Big Pebble: and Pitch It

Several years ago, Edward Mason opened a branch office in Boston for an advertising service that supplies prepared mats for retailers in the soft goods field. The company had no clients in the Boston market.

So Mason called first on a leading retailer who he knew was *not* a prospect, for the firm maintained a complete art department of its own. At this stage, Mason needed a ripple maker more than he needed a customer.

Note that he picked a *big pebble,* the top retailer in the field. *For the more prestigious the pebble the bigger the ripples.*

Now let Mason tell you in his own words how he used this first contact as the kickoff point for building one of his company's most successful branches.

"My approach was simple. I told him I was fully aware that his store could not use my services. 'But no one knows as many retailers in the Boston area as you do,' I added. Then I asked him if he would tell me which of those men would find my prepared mats most useful.

"His response was wonderful. He named more than a dozen men in that field who were 'comers' but whose stores were too small to have their own advertising departments. I wrote down the names, thanked him profusely, and left.

Step 2. Follow the Ripples

"In a few days I had called on each of these men. And I made one or two sales too. But I got something more from each one, the names of other prospects my first contact had not mentioned. Those names gave me more —and the ripples haven't stopped yet."

Two General Rules

The two steps above illustrate the pebble-in-the-pool technique. In addition, Mason's story highlights two important rules that apply to all the techniques.

a. Ask Them

"How did you get your 'pebbles' to give you those names?" I wanted to know, when Mason finished his story.

"Simple. I just asked them. Told them I was new in town, didn't know very many people, and would appreciate their help in getting to know the up-and-coming retailers."

Few, if any, contacts will volunteer names on their own. To start those ripples spreading—ask them.

b. Thank Them

Again Mason says it best. "Every time anyone gave me the name of another prospect, I thanked him. Then, after I made contact with the new name, I called the man who gave it to me and thanked him again.

"You'd be surprised how the word gets around. At the end of my first year we had five men in our Boston office. It all began with that first contact. What kept it going? What kept it going were those two words 'thank you.' "

2. The "Nest" Prospecting Technique

Working out of a "nest" produces excellent results for salesmen in many fields. How do you build a nest?

Start your selling with someone in an area or a group who can lead you to many others tied to him by a common bond, social, economic, or geographic.

Again, an example will best illustrate the technique.

Step 1. Pick Your Nest Builders

Recently I addressed a sales meeting of a firm with nearly 140 salesmen. During the discussion, I discovered that a quiet, somewhat elderly man was one of the firm's leading producers. After the meeting I asked him how he explained his success.

"That's easy," he said. "I work a 'nest' of prospects and customers that keeps me pretty busy."

"How did you develop this nest to begin with?"

"Well, it all started about 25 years ago. We sell a maintenance service to householders who heat their homes with oil or gas.

"I began working just an hour or two a few evenings a week, hanging on to my daytime office job. This was in my own neighborhood, so I knew who the most influential people were. Those who had a big circle of friends and were most respected.

Step 2. Sell Them On Service

"I figured that these were the people who could do me the most good—if I satisfied them. As soon as I made a sale I made a point of telling the customer he could count on me and my company when he needed service.

"Let me tell you, I worked at it. If the customer called me about a repair job, I got on to the office and had a serviceman there the next day. And I called the customer afterward to make sure everything was all right.

"The word began spreading: 'Let Fred Rounds take care of your furnace problems.' And the orders came in faster."

Step 3. Ask For Leads

"So that's it," I said. "You built your nest by word of mouth advertising."

"That was only part of it," Rounds replied. "Once my customers saw that I meant it about service, I started asking them for names of people who were good prospects for my service.

"Before the year was out, I was pulling in so much business that I gave up my office job. You see, Mr. Smith, a lot of salesmen are a little shy about asking their clients for prospects. They don't need to be if they come through on service."

There's no question about it. "Nest selling" works best when you consistently follow through after each sale.

3. The "Center of Influence" Technique

"Good selling takes a lot of know-how," says one experienced insurance man, "but whom you know can make up for a lot of gaps in what you know."

"If I call on one of my prospects as Bernard Koch of Prudential, I'll get a lot of 'not interested' responses. Yet many of those doors will swing open if I call as a man who's been referred to them by their minister, the town banker, or a well-known corporate attorney."

Anyone who is prominent enough and whose name commands respect can be used as a door-opening "center of influence." Most of us who sell know at least one such person well enough to turn to them for personalized leads. And we can cultivate others through our normal business contacts or by engaging in community service work.

Step 1. Sell Them

Because of their broad, general contacts, bankers, leading attorneys, accountants and management consultants are among the best types of "centers." But such men must be convinced that your service will benefit their customers or acquaintances before they will throw their names into the balance.

That defines your aim. Not to get them to buy, but to sell them on the value of your service.

Step 2. Help Them Help You

Most salesmen leave it to their "centers" to come up with referrals. But Jim Black, one of the top men in the business systems field, tells me that he gets his best results when he walks in with a previously prepared prospect list.

"You know." Jim says, "when you ask a busy banker, lawyer or accountant about prospects who might need more efficient office methods, it's tough for him to break off what he's doing and get his mind working on your problem. You've got to make it easy for them."

"Sounds logical, Jim. Tell me how you work it."

"Well, I just make out a list of people or firms I feel would be good prospects if I could get to them in the right way. Then I ask my 'center' if he knows any of them. I don't ask for introductions to all the names on the list—just the two or three the 'center' says he knows well."

Step 3. Ask Your "Center" to Introduce You

"From then on its simple. I just *ask for* a letter of introduction and get it nine times out of ten."

Here you go one step further than in the other prospecting techniques. You not only collect names—you get your "centers" to introduce you as well.

Jim Black says he's almost never been refused. Sometimes they may prefer to phone the prospect. But generally they favor an introductory letter.

Either way, the prestige of your "centers" carries over to you when they introduce you. "The prospect acts as though I'm almost as important as my 'center,' " Jim Black reports. "That's quite a help in a sale."

It certainly is. An "influence center" introduction is one of the strongest testimonials you can have.

Step 4. Say "Thank You" and Report Back

Since your center carries so much weight it would be a shame to use him on a one-shot basis. The best—and simplest—way of gaining his continued cooperation is to thank him for each introduction. And then let him know how the interview came out.

Everybody likes to help people. But nothing takes the glow off faster than having your helpful gesture taken for granted.

4. The "Endless Chain" Technique

You can't beat this method for producing a continuous supply of prospects, yet building a chain is simplicity itself. All you do is *request names from every person you interview*—whether you make the sale or not.

Nor need you limit your request to one name. A securities salesman who does a fine job of prospecting, tries to get six names from each person to whom he makes a sales presentation.

"It doesn't always work," he says. Then he adds with a grin, "But I'm always willing to settle for two or three."

a. When You've Made the Sale

The man who's just bought is bound to be high on your service. There's no better time to get his help on chain building.

And there's no better way than to ask him directly.

Here's how Cal Griffith does it out in Los Angeles.

"Mr. Saunders, could you give me the names of some friends who can also use our service—and might need it right now?"

That one straightforward appeal has helped him build an enviable volume of business.

"BETTER SERVICE" IS THE KEY

A few pages back, we saw how Fred Rounds builds selling "nests" by stressing service. Tom Fowler of Denver has become a fine "endless chain" builder by harping on service too.

No sooner does he complete the sale, Tom says, then "I tell him I'll keep in touch with him and will be available any time I am needed. Then I say something like this: 'If you have any friends who aren't getting that kind of service from their present supplier, I'd sure like to talk to them.'

"Right off most men will say they changed to me because they weren't getting good service elsewhere, and maybe so-and-so is feeling the same way. I almost always get two or three new prospects this way."

Sometimes the new client doesn't want his name used, for one reason or another. Naturally, you'll respect his wishes. But with or without permission to use his name, *ask him for prospects*.

b. When You've Been Turned Down

Some salesmen find it hard to ask for prospects from a man who's just said "no." Yet those who try it reap a harvest of names for their pains.

One man puts it this way: "I don't know what it is about such situations. Maybe they figure they'll get rid of me faster if they give me some names. Or maybe they feel I deserve it because of the work I put into the presentation.

"Whatever the reason, I've picked up hundreds of names since adopting the tactic of prospecting with every contact. And I've made many sales to *good* prospects that I got from prospects who turned me down."

5. The Client-to-Prospect Technique

In the "endless chain" technique you tap the enthusiasm of a new client. But who knows better than an *old* client exactly what your services can do for a friend.

A good salesman will contact an established customer at fairly regular intervals. Then why not schedule an occasional call as a *prospecting* visit?

Help Him Help You

Yes, this is the same tactic that pays off with "centers of influence." For your established customers may also be busy when you approach them for leads.

However, you can usually prepare a list of 10 or 15 people you think your customer might know. By asking him about those people specifically, you help him help you.

He's Your Best Prospect

Here at last is where the old adage fits. Your customer *is* your best prospect for other items in your line. When you're on a prospecting visit, you qualify *him* as a prospect for one or more items in your line you feel he might need, but may never have mentioned before.

A CLARIFICATION

Many of us look upon prospecting too narrowly: as a process of gathering names. Properly considered, to prospect is to search for *good* names—for people who might actually buy.

If every prospect you called on would buy, you'd wind up a millionaire in no time, but of course, it can never be like that. Try as hard as you may, you will never be able to zero in on the fruitful calls without wading through those which never materialize into sales.

Still, as long as you keep calling on prospects, on *potential customers,* you know you'll get your one sale out of five or whatever your average happens to be.

But what if you prepare and give a superb presentation only to find that your listener was never even a potential customer; had no need for your services, no money or no authority to buy? Then you've wasted your time completely. And as we shall see in the next chapter, most of us have too little actual selling time to waste.

That's why you want to reserve it for potential customers only.

The names you pick up in the first part of your prospecting program are only suspects: *potential prospects.* Should you make presentations to all these, you would hit only one out of 20 or 30 calls. Your previous selling time would be needlessly dissipated.

That's why the second step in prospecting, screening the suspects, sifting and sorting until only true prospects remain. What makes this both logical and productive is that it takes less time to screen each suspect than to prepare a sales presentation for him. This screening component we call *qualifying*.

3. HOW TO QUALIFY

Agreed: proper qualifying will help you concentrate your selling efforts where they will do the most good.

The point is: how do you isolate prospect from suspect?

Many methods suggest themselves. Essentially, however, any qualifying device is merely a variation on the one theme: putting the prospect to a three-pronged buying test.

Does he need your service?

Does he have the money or credit to buy?

Does he have the authority, the power to make the final buying decision?

If he fails in any one of these tests, you have a dead suspect. If he checks out on all, you have a live prospect.

Observe and Inquire

Sometimes qualifying requires personal contact with the suspect, sometimes not. Either way, the how of it boils down to two words: *observe* and *inquire*.

The question immediately arises: *where* do you look and *whom* do you ask? A modicum of thought will usually dictate the answers.

A visit to his address, for example, will give you an immediate line on his way of life: the kind of neighborhood, home or apartment he lives in; the kind of car he drives. And a friendly chat with a neighbor or local tradesman will reveal something about his family situation and perhaps offer a clue to his personal problems and needs.

Similarly, a visit to his office coupled with discreet inquiry among his employees or fellow workers, as the case may be, may uncover or hint at business problems your service could ameliorate.

Don't Make Like a Detective

Obviously, if you go about it in a way that makes the suspect feel you're tailing him or butting in on his private affairs—you can kiss the future sale goodby. A few people might be flattered by an investigation, but most will resent it. So the operative phrase: be discreet.

Nor should you let him know how much you've dug up on him. Keep the information inside your head, or better yet, put it on his file card. Having it will help you qualify him now and sell him later.

Of Time and Common Sense

As we have seen, the basic reason for qualifying is to reserve your precious selling time for those who are truly potential buyers. To expend too much time on qualifying in a given case would amount to little more than a meaningless robbing-Peter-to-pay-Paul charade.

Saving time is merely a matter of common sense: of knowing where to look and whom to ask, in the first place, and of when to stop in the second. Say your prospect must have a good credit rating; a quick look into Dun and Bradstreet might eliminate him immediately.

If you go about it right, you (or your secretary) can find out the exact nature of the suspect's work, get a fair approximation of his income, his credit rating, what schools his children attend, and the like. And all it may take are a few phone calls, the time to draft a letter or two, or a quick look in on his neighborhood.

Now let's get down to cases.

1. DRAW A PROSPECT "PROFILE"

To hit it big in selling intangibles, you must develop the habit of sizing up each suspect with whom you come into contact. The process must become so automatic that you do it without being consciously aware of it.

Building this habit will be faster—and surer in results—if you first draw a prospect "profile": fill in the outlines of the typical prospect for your services. Once you have fixed clearly in mind the key characteristics of a prospect, all you need do is match each new name against the "profile."

Who Is a Logical Prospect?

Certain features of your prospect "profile" can be fitted in from your experience and from the logic of your line. If your service is designed for homeowners, you'll automatically discard apartment dwellers.

If you're selling group insurance, you'll lop off one-man operators.

Two Examples

Home owner or renter? Businessman or professional? Married or single? Pre-school or college-age children? Executive or line employee?

Usually two or three of such general characteristics plus one or two specific to your field are enough to define your typical prospect. How they can be combined into a thumbnail sketch is illustrated by two examples.

Business Insurance

A business insurance salesman who has built up a comfortable income over the years finds that he can immediately eliminate as unsuitable those firms that do not conform to his prospect "profile."

"On the whole, I look for business firms that are successful and whose principals are probably insurable. The more successful the business, the greater the incentive to provide for its continuance.

"New firms," he says, "are not yet ripe. My prospects must be long established. And from experience I know they must range from a net worth of $30,000 to $2,000,000 to be worth a presentation."

Maintenance Service

One sales manager gives his men this simple "profile" to help cut down their qualifying time: "A prospect for our service is anyone who has a home with a central heating plant run on oil or gas and has the money in hand or can get an okay for a payment plan."

A "profile" with such broadly drawn strokes serves as a large-meshed strainer, quickly eliminating the more obvious misfits from your point of view. Not that you can rest content merely because the suspect measures up to this first check. But fewer will remain for sifting through a finer sieve.

2. DOES HE HAVE THE NEED?

Whatever intangibles you're selling, there must be some way they can meet the person's needs or solve a problem before you have the makings of a prospect. Even if he fits your general prospect "profile," you may want to be sure that he personally has a genuine need.

The Qualifying Interview

Here, pre-contact observation and inquiry can carry you just so far. To check him out you may have to ask directly—by phone or face-to-face.

Many prefer the phone, since you can qualify in minutes, where face-to-face checking might take hours of travel time and waiting.

"I wouldn't do it any other way," says Pat Hughes. "I can pick up the phone and say: 'Mr. Wilson, this is Pat Hughes of United Insurance. You don't know me, but your friend Art Goodman suggested that I talk to you about our cut rate automobile insurance. Would you mind telling me when your current policy expires?'

"In one minute I determine if I have a live prospect or a dead suspect."

Two Pointers

Besides saving time, Pat's telephone technique illustrates two other factors in good qualifying. To begin with, he referred back to the customer who gave him the lead to Mr. Wilson. This is always good practice; they'll listen more closely and sympathetically when you've been referred by a friend.

Secondly, he slipped in a slight but definite sales message: " . . . our *cut rate* insurance." True, you're not there to sell—you just want to see if it's worthwhile making a presentation later.

But a brief mention of benefits can help create a need. In some cases, if the prospect's reaction so warrants, it can open the way to an immediate presentation.

Creating a Need

Pat Hughes took only a second. In the next case, the salesman does a good job of creating the need while qualifying the prospect.

"Mrs. Powers, this is Lester Bascomb, with the Watertown Painting and Decorating Company. I'm calling to let you know that we're giving local homeowners a 25% discount on our services during the slack season. Tell me, Mrs. Powers, how long have you owned your home?"

"We've lived here more than 15 years."

"I can certainly see why. That is a fine neighborhood with a *lot of attractively decorated homes.* May I ask how long it has been since you had your home painted?"

"It's been about seven years or more."

"Then I'm glad I called you, Mrs. Powers; *we find it's best not to wait much longer than that.*"

"Maybe you're right. But you'll have to talk to my husband about that."

The *italicized* sentences, of course, illustrate the way Bascomb mixed selling with his qualifying. And the call didn't take much longer than the previous one described. Besides, Bascomb swept right on to make an appointment to see husband and wife together.

And that raises another point. Once you've qualified the prospect, you can always effect a transition to a pre-approach—making your selling appointment then and there.

3. DOES HE HAVE THE MONEY, OR THE CREDIT?

How you check the capacity to pay will depend on whether you sell to business firms or to individuals. When qualifying firms, the simplest and fastest way is to use one of the credit rating services, such as Dun and Bradstreet. Their services are available to any reputable company.

Try Their Competitors or Suppliers

Some firms are not listed by any rating bureau. But you can often accomplish the same result—and almost as quickly—by querying the company's suppliers or competitors.

Not that such sources freely hand out information to anyone who comes along with a direct question of this sort. However, a casual inquiry will often do the trick.

Like this one: "How are things going at Acme Plastics these days?"

Chambers of Commerce and Associations

Local Chambers of Commerce or business associations to which the prospect firm belongs generally have much valuable information. True, the people you contact in such organizations will rarely make any critical comment. However, the way they speak or the deliberate avoidance of a direct answer may often be a cue to a bad prospect.

Your Friends or Clients

Don't overlook the help you might get from present clients or friends in the same industry as the firm you are qualifying. In most cases they will be glad to supply any information they may have.

Banks

Salesmen could use banks as a source of information on business firms far more than they do, according to Charles Kingston who specializes in office systems. "Just by asking an employee," he says, "I can usually find out easily enough where the firm does its banking. Most bankers want to protect their current loans and get business loans; so they will cooperate in discreet inquiry. They don't give me all the details, but I get enough information to determine if they have the capacity to buy."

QUALIFYING INDIVIDUALS

As noted before, inquiry into individual capacity to pay will most often start in the neighborhood. Once again, the make car he buys, the home he lives in, the clothes he wears will give you your first clues.

Many intangibles salesmen find that local tradespeople, such as grocers, gas station operators and the like, are voluble suppliers of information. As one of the leading mutual funds salesmen in the country once remarked to me: "If some of my prospects ever knew how much I was digging up on them from local dealers, they would probably never buy in their own neighborhoods again!"

On the Telephone

Capacity to pay inquiry may often have to be directed at the suspect himself. This can be done quickly enough via phone; just make sure you don't do it in a way that gets his back up.

To avoid this, experiment with your qualifying questions until you're sure you hit on one that gives no offense—and that you can rely on to produce an honest answer. Then stay with it.

Phillip Holmes, for example, after much trial and error, finds that the following questions will make or break the possibility of a sale.

"If you're reasonably certain in your mind, Mr. Kaslow, that this investment program is everything I claim it to be, are you in a financial position to take advantage of it *now*—even on a small scale?"

4. DOES HE HAVE THE AUTHORITY?

Beginning salesmen especially tend to waste too much time selling to purchasing agents merely because they're the ones who sign the final purchasing order. But the *decision* to buy is often initiated by officials in other departments.

Who's the Big Wheel?

You'll be dollars ahead when you know who has the real buying authority for your services. Rarely will a purchasing agent pretend to be an authority on services which engineers or art directors, let us say, wish to buy.

Ask him who's authorized to put the requisition through. Then try to sell him on the idea of arranging an appointment for you with that man. You'll not only track down the man with the real authority—but you'll have a personalized introduction to him, which always helps.

He Does It by Phone

Richard Farleigh, who handles an expensive business service, makes most of his appointments in advance by phone. Although he has his calls routed to the purchasing office, he knows that in most cases the real buying authority lies elsewhere.

Farleigh makes no bones about wanting to speak to the man who really decides. "Mr. Craig," he says, "I appreciate your willingness to let me show you our plan, *but before I accept and take up your time and mine,* can you tell me if the decision about such things is entirely up to you?" (While he goes directly to the heart of the matter, Farleigh carefully couches his questions so as to imply a mutual gain in referring him to the right party.)

Should the answer be "no," Farleigh goes on just as candidly. "In that case, Mr. Craig, I would appreciate it if you would see to it that anyone else involved in this decision is present when I come to see you tomorrow afternoon."

"Don't they feel you're being somewhat high handed?" I asked.

"Very seldom. In part, they seem to respect me more. If they should hesitate to go along with my request, I make the point again.

"Please understand me, Mr. Craig," I'll say. "Your time is valuable and so is mine. I don't want to waste either yours or mine by having to repeat my story to different people at different times.

"Besides, someone who is directly involved may think of questions or special problems you might not have thought of. That's why I think it would be to your advantage as well as mine to have everyone involved in the decision present when I make my presentation."

Farleigh agrees that this hard sell qualifying might not suit everyone's temperament. But when I asked: "Do you feel that you ever lost an in-interview that you might have had except for this method?" he countered with an emphatic "no."

"Don't be afraid to insist that the man you are going to see actually has the power of decision. You may think he might take offense—but he almost never does. Actually, as I said before, he respects me for it."

Watch For the Clues

In many business sales, more than one principal will be present for the interview. Rarely do they share equally in making the buying decision. By looking for cues (or investigating beforehand) you can generally spot, and focus on, the power figure.

But play it cool. If you cut the other party out too openly, you may offend him. And while he may lack buying power, he may well have *veto* power.

Aware of this factor, Boris Taimanov is invariably courteous if his qualifying question gets a negative response. Generally, Taimanov gets an office manager on the phone. "My firm," he'll say, "has developed a specialized service that has proven very popular with businessmen here. I'd like to know if you're the man to speak to about it. That is, do you make the decision on office service requisitions?"

"I'm afraid not."

"Well, in any case, can I send you our free booklet? You might find it helpful."

"Sure, send it along."

"Okay, I'll have it in the mails for you today. By the way, can you tell me who has the say on services that are exclusively for office use?"

That last question, or something like it, should be an automatic follow-up to a negative response.

Make It a Family Affair

The intangibles salesman with long experience in the personal field doesn't have to be told that the same rule applies here: find the buying authority. If you think it's Mr. Bailey who makes the buying decisions in the Bailey family, you may be in for a shock. In these days of women's liberation, especially—the woman ignored may be the "no sayer."

In most cases, the safest thing to do is to arrange a joint interview. One man who's up near the top in the life insurance business refuses to give a presentation unless the wife will be present.

"It's her businss too," he insists. "Even if the husband claims to be the big wheel in the family, she'll resent being left out of it. That's bound to hurt in the long run."

Use a Check List

Because the qualifying procedure determines how many suspects finally make your prospect file and, ultimately, how productive your selling time may be, you might find it wise to develop a check list of questions under each factor: need, capacity to buy, authority to buy.

In each case I give a starter list. With a little thought, you can add questions most appropriate to your selling situation.

1. Does This Prospect Need What I Am Selling?

a) Does he have personal or business problems my service might ease?
b) Can I save him money by selling him this service?
c) Can I help him make money with this service?
d) Can I help him do his job better?
e) Can I make his future more secure?

2. Does He Have the Money to Buy?

a) Have I checked with people who know this individual or firm well enough to know the economic condition?
b) Have I checked his credit rating?

3. Does This Prospect Have the Power to Buy?

a) Will he have to consult with others before buying?
b) Will the decision be a group decision?
c) Is there any hint that a silent partner is involved?

The questions you add should refer specifically to the type of things you'd need to know in your particular line. You'll save a lot of selling time for the buyers who can really use your services if you check each lead out in terms of these questions before adding him to your prospect file.

5. HOW TO MANAGE YOUR PROSPECT FILE

You've squeezed out your suspects, added your new prospects to your files. Now you want to work them to best advantage. That takes good management in three basic areas.

1. Classify your prospects.
2. Keep good records.
3. Age your prospect files regularly.

1. CLASSIFY YOUR PROSPECTS

All your prospects have qualified equally—but some are more equal than the others, to coin a cliche. So you divide them into categories that help you determine—

1. When you will call on a given prospect.
2. How often you will call on him.
3. How long you will keep him in your prospect file.

How To Rate Your Accounts

The classifications you set up will depend on your needs and whether you work a one or two interview system. However you do it, you'll make more sales in the long run by following the basic rule: Give each prospect a rating.

1. You May Rate Them by Need

Some prospects have a pressing need for your service and are on the verge of buying. So you assign them an "A" rating for immediate follow-up.

Others you grade as "B" or "C" depending on how readily you think you can convert them into buyers. Salesmen who follow this system may call on all their "A's," then the "B's," and so on down the line.

Those who work the two-interview system may often adopt a variation of this method. They also set up three classifications:

A. Those who can be sold quickly.
B. Those who are not ready to buy now but can be developed into buyers with minimum effort.
C. Those who might be developed into buyers after intensive cultivation.

The top-rated prospects they might try to sell in a one-interview presentation—provided they have enough information on the prospect besides his urgency of need.

The middle group will be set up for the usual exploratory call plus selling follow-up.

For the "C's," they will schedule a longer series of fact-finding and cultivation calls before attempting to close. How long this cultivation will continue rests on the profit potential.

2. Rate On Volume and Profit Potential

The object here is to determine how many calls each prospect may be worth. This poses a problem, for many intangibles salesmen make it a hard and fast rule never to call twice on a prospect. If they can't sell him, that's it.

Personally, I think this is shortsighted; besides, it's unfair to the salesman and prospect both. Even if you or your firm insist on this rule, a bit of flexibility surely makes sense. Otherwise you rule out many a potential high volume buyer needlessly.

In any case, ratings in this category are generally based on three factors:

1. The probable volume should the account be cracked.
2. The possibility of repetitive sales.
3. The likelihood that a small buyer of today will be a big buyer of tomorrow.

The better your record-keeping system, the more productive your prospect file. A good system is one that keeps the essential facts on each prospect in convenient, easy-to-use form, simplifies updating, and lets you tell at a glance what kind of prospecting, selling, or follow-up effort is needed at any moment of time.

The amount and kind of desired data will vary with the salesman and the service he sells. Generally speaking, however, a good system will spotlight three main kinds of facts:

1. Those that enable you to qualify prospects promptly and effectively.
2. Those that guide you in making an effective sales presentation.
3. Those that help you classify prospects for various follow-up purposes.

2. AGE YOUR PROSPECT FILES

You cannot sell them all. No matter how well-qualified a person may be to use the services you offer, or no matter how badly you think he may need those services—you may still never get him to close the deal.

For you, then, that well-qualified prospect is just a dud.

All of us in the selling game occasionally slide into a slump because we work a tighter and tighter circle of prospects who don't buy. How can you avoid getting into this condition?

There's one best way. Sit down periodically and age your prospect list, eliminating those that go beyond a certain time—no matter how well qualified they are otherwise.

How Long Should You Keep a Prospect Alive?

Every salesman will swear by a different aging formula. Once you've worked out the one that seems best suited to *your* circumstances, you've got to apply it ruthlessly—tossing out of your files every name that has overstayed its welcome.

Here are three examples that show how widely formulas may vary. More to the point, they show why you must work out your own. For what's good for one man may be poison for another.

A Long Haul—and a Profitable One

Would you cultivate a prospect for five years? This man did.

"It took five years to the day to get my first contract with this organization. Once even my boss told me not to make any more calls, but I knew I'd eventually get this business—and I did. All the time and effort expended has been more than repaid in the short three years we have now had the contract."

Where the unit of sale is large or the long range potential exceptionally good, such persistent cultivation may pay off. But this man's formula?

"I set no absolute time. But if I feel it's been going on long enough, I'll call another salesman in to try. If he gets nowhere, I tear up my notes and records on the case and forget about it."

A Two-Year Limit

Pete Reynolds puts it flatly: "If I don't get some business from a prospect in a two-year period, I stop calling."

And it works out fine—for him.

He Gives Them Four Rounds

A friend of mine who sells a service to banks, covers his territory three times a year. This means that he sees his prospects at intervals of about four months.

Here's his formula:

"No matter how big the order might be, if I don't get it in the third or fourth time round, I scratch my prospect from my list. In my business I figure they know me by my fourth call and know my service. If they don't buy by this time, then I'd better call on someone else."

SUMMARY

Every so often, stop and check up on your prospecting system.

Are you following a definite plan? Is it as good as you can make it? Do you do some prospecting every day? Do you conscientiously apply one or more of the time-tested techniques for getting personalized referrals?

Are you applying the right criteria in qualifying prospects? Have you clearly defined your typical prospect? Do you use the telephone often enough to qualify prospects?

Have you worked out a rating system for those in your prospect file? Do you keep good records? Do you age your prospect file periodically? Do you follow a definite formula when so doing?

Your answers to these questions should indicate where review or more intensive application is necessary.

2

How to Manage

Your Selling Time Effectively

According to an extensive McGraw-Hill study, the typical salesman spends on the average only 40% of his working time with customers and prospects. Indeed, many experienced sales managers say this overstates the case because it doesn't take waiting time into account.

For example, the sales manager of the Emory Air Freight Express estimates actual face-to-face selling time at only two hours a day: or less than 500 hours a year. For the salesman who earns $15,000 and has expenses of $5,000, the value of each selling hour comes to over $40.

While these figures may vary from man to man, one thing remains constant. Good time management can spell the difference between outstanding and mediocre performance.

We shall consider the ways and means of effective time management under two broad headings:

1. Make your selling time more productive.
2. Squeeze more selling hours out of your working day.

Let us consider each area in turn.

A. MAKE YOUR SELLING TIME MORE PRODUCTIVE

When he contemplates all the things he must do to make his calls effective and then considers the limited time at his disposal, many a salesman has fervently wished for a 26-hour day.

If you can't make the day longer, you can make it more productive. How?

You can spend more of your time where it counts the most. You can walk into each interview better prepared to make your sale. You can allot more time to prospecting and development selling.

1. SPEND YOUR TIME WHERE IT COUNTS THE MOST

To get the highest possible yield out of every selling hour, you must invest your time where the potential for sales and earnings is greatest. Most salesmen have more customers and prospects than they can effectively cultivate. And all too often a representative will burn up shoe leather attempting to give equal coverage to every account—when he could be spending more time with the more productive ones.

While some customers are regular buyers at a volume commensurate with their incomes, others buy less frequently and in smaller amounts. And if some prospects can be converted to customers quickly, others may be too time-consuming to be worth the required investment of time.

As studies have shown, as many as 4/5 of the sales are made to as few as 1/5 of the customers. Indeed, one brokerage house has found that the salesmen who were making the fewest calls per day were recording the largest volume of sales.

Why?

Because these men were following a calling plan based on carefully calculated productivity estimates. By devoting more time to the better prospects, they were closing more sales.

It comes down to this: *To cultivate your territory most productively, the quality of your calls becomes more vital than the quantity.*

a. Develop a Cream-Separating Device

There are several ways of planning the best use of your time. Here is one of the simplest: Identify each account and prospect as "A," "B," "C," or "D" in accordance with present importance and future potential. Then schedule your calling frequency accordingly.

Every salesman does this to some degree. But in my experience, those who adopt a more formal cream-separating device boost their sales volume higher and faster than those who do it haphazardly.

HE MAKES FEWER CALLS—BUT BETTER ONES

Gene Ruppert, one of the top producers of an office systems organization, draws up a master rating and frequency schedule every year. He begins by placing his customers and prospects into high, medium or low dollar volume categories, based on actual records in the one case, and his knowledge of the field, in the other. Then he balances the time he spent with each account over the year against the actual or anticipated results.

Weighing these factors—present customer volume, customer and prospect potential, and invested selling time—according to values determined by his cost and profitability circumstances, he pinpoints the overall amount of time he will spend on a given account for the coming year.

Grading an account is not simply a matter of current volume, Gene points out. Thus a low-volume customer (or even a non-buyer) with heavy volume or profit prospects may be rated higher than a high-volume buyer whose business is on the decline.

Once the ratings have been settled to Gene's satisfaction, each account is slotted into a corresponding calling schedule. That is, the "A" accounts are called upon once a week, the "B" accounts every two weeks, the "C" accounts monthly.

Originally, Gene had established a "D" category to be called on quarterly. But an analysis of his time inventory convinced him that he could not hope to follow through on his proposed schedule and still maintain the desired quality of presentations. This faced him with an important policy decision.

Should he lengthen the time between calls? Or should he cut out certain customers and prospects?

Gene decided to eliminate the marginal accounts and focus on the most productive ones, instead. That is, he held on to an "A," "B," "C" schedule —cutting out all "D" customers and prospects.

In the five years since he hooked on to this cream-separating device, Gene's volume and earnings have moved up steadily. He credits the increase almost wholly to this practice of concentrating his time where it counts the most.

LET THE CATEGORIES FIT YOUR CIRCUMSTANCES

As the man who manages your territory, you are in the best position to determine how many categories you want to establish, how to go about doing it, and what calling frequencies you should follow.

A brokerage salesman, for example, might place his heavy traders in the "A" category, and phone each "A" man once a day to keep him well informed on market trends and the condition of his holdings.

Under the "B" umbrella, he might group his regular investors—those who come in for growth or income every week. In this case, the volume wouldn't matter: the $100 one would rate as high as the $5,000 one—so long as both were regular weekly investors. These "B" customers would come in for once a week contacts.

The "C's" would be just as regular as the "B" customers, but they would invest less frequently, perhaps monthly, and might be called on a monthly basis as well.

In this business, the experienced salesman might well establish a "D" category: the irregular investor who has a fine potential for growth. He might be called every three or four months.

In the insurance field, your category slottings would be determined by your specialty: life insurance, casualty and fire, or business. And your calling schedules would be established accordingly.

However you do it, the cream-separating classifications should fit *your* situation, square with *your* judgement.

REVIEW AND REVISE

You can never do a perfect job of cream separating. For as conditions change, categories will change. The "A" account of today may well be the "D" account of tomorrow, and vice versa. This underscores the need to review and revise your ratings from time to time in the light of new information.

As one man writes: "Since time is money and selling time is limited, I reclassify my customers quarterly. On a quarterly basis only a few changes need be made—but each one adds up in time saved and extra money earned."

HANDLING THE MARGINAL ACCOUNT

Whatever categories you set up, you will eventually come down to the marginal accounts—those which pose the inevitable dilemma: should I keep them, or dump them?

In the example cited above, Gene Ruppert sloughed off his "D" customers and prospects because for him the cost of cultivating their business —in terms of excess time investment—was too high.

Given the circumstances, his decision was justified. Yet many of today's biggest volume outlets started out as marginal accounts in the past. And since you can't always measure their growth potential accurately, it pays to find a way to maintain contact with some marginal accounts without eating too deeply into your precious selling time.

To this end, some salesmen establish a special "telephone contact" category for certain marginal prospects who can be called as fill-ins when regularly-scheduled calls must be cancelled. Again, whether or not it pays to attempt even such minimal contacts with "D" or "E" category prospects and customers depends upon your special circumstances.

CREAM SEPARATING BY TERRITORY

A number of salesmen report good results from cream separating by sales areas, rather than by individual customers. First they evaluate different *parts* of their territories by sales potential. Then they determine how intensively they will cultivate each part.

Frank Walke tells an interesting story of how it worked for him. "Some time ago," he says, "my firm had a sales consultant go out into the field with me. I started beefing to him about my territory being too small. 'I can't find enough decent prospects,' I insisted. The man said nothing to this, but I noticed him clocking my calls for the rest of the day.

"After dinner that night, he finally took up the point. 'Frank,' he said, 'the way I worked it out you don't spend *enough time* with each prospect to do a really good job on him. Look,' he went on, 'here's a local road map. Would you spot your present buyers and prospects on this map?'

"When I finished, he showed me how these clustered in certain areas, with a few lone buyers sprinkled out here and there by themselves. Then he said something that really rocked me. 'If you *cut* your territory instead of extending it—and concentrate your calls where you have the heaviest grouping of customers and prospects, you'll get all the additional business you've been wanting.'

"Well, I didn't go for it right away, but it kept working on my mind. Finally I figured I had nothing to lose by trying it. First I picked seven areas where I had the heaviest groupings. Then, checking back over my records, I listed them according to profitability. I also considered such factors as servicing costs and travel time before I stabilized the listings.

"By cutting my territory down to size and allocating my time to each area according to profitability, I can now devote more time to my important customers. Besides, with enough time to cultivate those who are small on the books but big in potential, I find I can actually realize that potential in a good percentage of the cases."

b. Talk To the Right Man

Any salesman who has been in the field for any length of time will agree that he spends too much time with people who turn out to lack the power of decision and can do little to further the sale.

True, when selling intangibles, it is often necessary to cultivate many people who can be helpful, even though they can't decide. These helpful "assistants" may range upon occasion from secretaries and telephone operators to executive vice presidents.

For all that, when you fail to find out who the decision-makers are and get to them reasonably soon, you lose precious time and often the business as well.

Who has the authority to buy? Will the man I am seeing have to consult with others before buying? Will the decision to buy in this case be a group decision? Is there reason to suspect that there is a silent partner who must be consulted?

Whether selling to business firms or individuals, the trick is to work up a checklist of questions like these to help you determine who is the right person or persons to deal with. Such a checklist can be a significant time saver. More important, it will help you invest your time where it counts the most.

2. GO IN PREPARED

If anything is certain in selling, this is it: The salesman who starts his day knowing on whom he plans to call and what he plans to discuss in each interview will make more effective calls, cover more ground in less time, and write more orders than the salesman who neglects such pre-planning.

Know Your Prospects and Customers

Preparation begins with building your customer file. "From your very first call on your prospect," says one seasoned representative, "you've got to start learning what matters most to *him*. In my own case, I put together a folder on each account, using white folders for customers, colored ones for prospects.

"My folders keep me up-to-date on every prospect's interests and on customer orders and servicing requirements. After each call I record what selling points they responded to, what, if anything, they bought, and what they might buy next time. This has been of great value as a time saver and selling tool. Because a glance at the folder just before the interview helps me shape up my presentation mentally, I can get right to the point without wasting his time or mine."

"I Take a Mental Drive Every Morning"

"In the big cities, most stock and bonds transactions are conducted by phone. But in small towns and rural areas, a lot of business is done on a face-to-face basis. One top producer in the mid-west swears by his long-established practice of post-breakfast preparation.

"After my breakfast coffee," he says, "I take a mental drive through my territory, with pad and pencil at hand. I think of each buyer in the order I plan to see him that day, recalling with the aid of a notebook our last meeting.

"Did I promise any information or research reports that I have not yet provided? What new offerings have I heard of that will be of special interest to him? Shall I attempt to sell him this time or would it be wiser to explore his situation further? Is he ripe for a monthly investment plan? How can I plant the seed of the idea?

"As I pose these and other questions to myself, the scheme of each interview gradually unfolds. By getting my story across in shorter time, that hour of preparation helps me squeeze in an extra call or two almost every day."

When Is Enough?

How much time should you invest in preparation?

"Enough" for one call, may be too much or too little for another. Your own knowledge of prospect potential must guide you. In this connection, one salesman gets additional mileage out of his preparation time by tying it to his cream-separating categories.

"Since classifying my accounts," he tells me, "I have been taking more time to prepare constructive, in-depth presentations for all my 'A' accounts and some of my 'B's.' This has paid off in more regular repeat business."

"What about your other categories?" I asked.

"Well, I'd like to do the same for my 'C' and 'D' customers too. But there are just so many hours to work with, so they get more routine presentations."

On the Telephone, Too

In face-to-face selling, you can stop to light a cigarette when you need time to size up an unexpected complication. Or you can root around in your bag for pertinent data without irritating the prospect.

On the phone a minute of silence stretches out forever. You can lose many a sale by keeping a man dangling on a dead wire while you scuttle around for information you should have assembled in advance. Silence may be golden elsewhere, but on the phone it's fatal.

Organize Your Desk

Actually, the telephone salesman has an edge here, for he can have far more information at his fingertips than the outside salesman can carry in his briefcase.

That is, he can *if* he organizes his desk for it.

Certainly such things as research reports, market trend charts, condition of customer holdings, and the like can be right at your desk and well organized for easy reference. One man insists that time invested in preparation the night before pays handsome dividends in extra productivity.

"When you use the phone six hours a day, you feel you'll never have enough time to attend to all the little details that arise. Recently, I started making out my calling list the night before. Once I have my calling schedule worked out, I pull my file cards for each man on the list: going over all my notations of previous conversations and transactions. Then, on a separate sheet of paper, I outline the recommendations I'm going to make the next day and the selling points I want to get across.

"I keep the cards and attached sheet on my desk in alphabetical order. Before I pick up the receiver for each call, it's easy to run through the material for a quick review. Usually, I have enough there to answer any questions the prospect may raise."

Have a Specific Reason for Calling

In any kind of selling, the here-I-am-again call—the call whose only purpose is to remind the prospect that you're still alive and well—is an irritating time-waster. On the phone, it's poison.

For there's an urgency about a ringing phone that produces a decided let down when one finds a salesman on the other end who's calling "just to say hello."

As an insurance man writes: "You're wasting your time if you phone without a definite purpose. Even worse, you're wasting the prospect's time."

Plan your call around an idea which will *help* the customer in some way, or around an offer you're sure will interest him. Or plan it as a quick exploratory call, with an appointment-seeking close, like this:

"I thought you'd be interested in something I just got a line on from our research department. Would you like me to send you a digest of their report?"

If he says "yes" follow up with: "I'll call you next week after you've had a chance to think about it."

If he says "no" you've still made a *constructive* contact. The message: you really take his interests to heart.

3. ALLOT MORE TIME TO PROSPECTING

Although we discuss the prime importance of prospecting in Chapter 3, the subject rates an additional, if brief, emphasis here. For as an intangibles salesman, you are *not* managing your time to greatest effect unless you allow a minimum of 20% for prospecting.

You are most productive as a salesman when you are actively opening new accounts, cultivating new prospects and increasing your share of existing markets. The more you maximize this part of your selling time, the more you and your firm stands to gain.

This brings us to the second phase of effective time management:

B. SQUEEZE MORE SELLING HOURS OUT OF YOUR WORKING DAY

Recently I helped a friend make a time analysis of a large sale. Averaging his commission against this record of time spent in swinging the deal, it turned out that he had earned $40 an hour for the time directly spent on that sale.

"But my average sale pays me over $100 an hour, Abbott," he exclaimed. "I must have been nuts to spend so much time on this one."

"No, Jim, I don't think so," I said. "You see, you forget the hours *behind* your $100 an hour average sale. Do you figure in the hours engaged in prospecting, planning, travel, desk time—and maybe a few long 'entertainment lunches' too?"

Jim's reaction illustrates how important it is to have an accurate account of the amount of time spent on different aspects of your job—from organizing your desk to waiting for your prospect to see you or get to the phone. And there's something more involved than averaging your hourly income per sale.

As a salesman, your actual selling time—face-to-face or on the phone—

represents your major working capital. Like all capital, it should be conserved, built up where possible, and invested wisely.

Good time management means *squeezing more selling hours* out of your working day—while paring to the bone time invested in other directions. Sufficient time must also be allocated to direct supporting activities: reading and research, preparing constructive presentations, prospecting, and the like. But a well-planned time budget makes provisions for these in ways that leave your actual selling-time "capital" virtually intact.

Some activities represent a pure waste of that capital: travel and waiting time, to mention only the two most obvious ones. While such time drains cannot be lopped off completely, they can be cut down to size.

How you do it will be covered under the following headings:

1. Prepare a time budget.
2. Develop a time control plan.
3. Plan your travel and routing schedules.
4. Plan fill-in activities beforehand.
5. Put a ceiling on waiting time.
6. Use the appointment method.
7. Sleep where you'll work.

1. PREPARE A TIME BUDGET

A survey of 255 salesmen in 19 different fields shows that on the average, a salesman's working day breaks down as follows:

Getting ready to sell: planning, gathering information, prospecting	1.7 hours
Traveling, waiting time, lunch	4.2 hours
Keeping records and other paper work	.7 hours
Actual selling (interviews)	2.7 hours
Total	9.3 hours

When I discussed these findings with a friend of mine who specializes in casualty and fire insurance, he wouldn't believe the figures applied to him. But two weeks after I induced him to run a time check on himself, he told me: "Abbott, I was amazed to find I was averaging only a little more than two hours a day talking to prospects. That bothered me. So yesterday I got down to planning my day and I figured out literally a dozen ways of adding more actual selling time to the day's schedule."

The moral is clear. Before you can squeeze more selling hours out of your working day, you must first become time conscious.

Keep a Time Record

How much time do you spend in the office during selling hours? How much of it is essential to your work? Do your lunch and coffee breaks cut into prime selling time too much? Are you using a considerable amount of prime time on non-selling activities that could be reduced or eliminated?

You just can't find out where your time goes and how it might be more productively budgeted, without keeping a formal time chart for a week or two. With your figures in hand, you can better allocate your "time-capital" expenditures, maximizing your selling and selling support activities, cutting down sharply on the time wasters.

Nor need this analysis be complicated.

Start on a Monday. Jot down in a notebook *everything* you do each working day from 9 a.m. to 5 p.m.

Put down the exact time you get into the field or pick up your phone for the first time. Note each moment devoted to travel, waiting, preparing, reading, interviewing, prospecting time. Show when and how long you have lunch, how many coffee breaks and how long, how much time you put into record keeping.

Remember: this is for *yourself*. If you shave your time wasting figures, you're only cheating yourself.

At the end of the week or two of record keeping, all that remains are simple arithmetic calculations. Once you have your actual time expenditures charted, you are ready to draw up a time budget that will do the best job for you. Additional suggestions on this will present themselves as we move along in this section.

2. DEVELOP A TIME CONTROL PLAN

Your time budget is as good as your follow through. And as in all budgeting, follow through depends on planned controls.

The $25,000 Idea

Finding a salesman who doesn't plan the use of his time to some extent would be a pretty hopeless job. The point is: how well does he do it—and how consistently?

When Charles Schwab headed Bethlehem Steel, he granted an interview one day to the famed public relations consultant, Ivy Lee. "We have more things that should be done every day," said Schwab, "than either I or my staff can ever get to. What we need is not more new ideas, but more ways of doing what we already know.

"Show me a way to do these things in less time," Schwab continued, "and if it works, I'll pay anything within reason you bill me for."

After thinking this over, Lee replied: "I have a method that will increase your personal management efficiency—and that of everyone else who applies it, by as much as 50%."

Handing Schwab a blank piece of paper, he said, "Write down the most important things you must do tomorrow."

That took Schwab about five minutes.

"Now number them in the order of their true importance to you and the firm."

This took somewhat longer: Schwab wanted to be sure he had it right.

"Okay," said Lee. "You're all set. First thing in the morning look at item one. Start working on it—*and stay with it until it's done.* That way, you'll do it in the least possible time.

"Then take on item two; when that's finished, move on to three, and so on down the line. If you can't finish every item on your list, don't worry about it. For there's no other way you could.

"Those that are truly important you can reschedule for the next day, moving them up the line. Those that are not, you can forget about completely.

"But with this method, the things that get done are those which have the greatest real value for you and your company. Do this every working day; have your men do it too. Try it as long as you like. Then send me your check for whatever you think the idea is worth."

After two months, Charles Schwab sent Ivy Lee a $25,000 check for this time-control plan. Many years later, he wrote: "That was the most profitable $25,000 I spent in my entire business career."

You can try it for nothing.

Says one man who did: "The best thing that happened was that I eliminated many chores I found weren't necessary at all. This gave me more time for the three things that matter most to me: making more calls; putting in more prospecting time; keeping on top of market trends."

Making Time to Prepare

Every salesman agrees that preparation and planning would improve his sales-to-calls ratio, but practically all will groan, "I can't find the time for it."

With a time-control plan, you will—and it needn't cut into your precious selling time either.

One representative reports that the Ivy Lee plan has helped him carve out two hours a night for productive preparation. "To pay off most profitably," he writes, "a day spent calling on customers and prospects should be preceded by a couple of hours of preparation.

"But like every salesman, I found this impossible to do. However, by following the first-things-first method, I now manage to put in two hours of preparation most evenings without any strain."

Time-Control for Reading

In most intangibles fields, a certain amount of literature must be studied intensively. Other reading, such as trade papers, may be skimmed through more casually—provided you pause to digest those items which can serve you well.

Here again we run smack up against the problem of time management. Knowing that a given booklet or article has important information that can be profitably applied almost immediately is one thing. The tough job is finding time to read it.

One highly successful salesman who must work against tough competition divides the reading material which comes his way into three piles: must read; read if possible; throw out.

He schedules his "must" reading carefully—setting aside 30 minutes every morning. That way, he never lets it get too far ahead of him.

He wades through a fair amount of the "read if possible" pile at odd moments of the day. If it starts stacking up, he transfers much of it to the "throw out" file.

By rationalizing his reading in this manner, he tells me: "I've compiled a wealth of information my competitors don't even know about."

You'll be further ahead of the game if you follow the lead of a number of salesmen who compile "information notebooks." Clip, copy and file items of special interest to you or your prospects. Carefully indexed under descriptive headings, such a personal information file can prove to be one of your most profitable time investments.

Make A Plan and Work It

Your time control plan for preparation and reading must be *yours,* designed to fit *your* needs, *your* temperament, *your* schedule. Make the plan modest enough so that you can carry it through practically—but make it!

Make It a Habit. No matter how much or how little time you allocate for preparation and study—set aside a definite day or definite hour for it and form the habit of following through at that time come hell or high water.

For what counts is regularity. Adding a little more preparation or knowledge every day or every week mounts up in terms of extra sales.

3. PLAN YOUR TRAVEL AND ROUTING SCHEDULE

Better travel-time management can increase your active selling time *with no increase in working hours.*

Consider. A Carnegie Institute study reveals that 60% of a salesman's time is taken up in getting from one prospect to another and in reception rooms. The less distance you travel and the more carefully you route yourself to avoid criss-crossings, the more calls you make—and the more sales. It's truly as simple as that.

Planning Your Route

No matter how large or small your territory, you can save traveling time by investing a few minutes in planning your route. Just two steps need be followed.

a. *Concentrate Your Calls In The Morning And Again In The Afternoon.*
Some salesmen build such concentrated schedules around key calls or interviews. On any given day your calling schedule will include one or more individuals or firms whom you especially want to see. They may be new leads; they may have granted you definite appointments; they may be ready for closing interviews.

Following this routing method, you locate these key calls on a street or road map. Then you build two call groupings around them—one for the morning, one for the afternoon.

One representative says: "The grouping method gives me a good idea of where I'll be at lunch time. That way I can often arrange to have lunch with an important prospect or customer. Scheduling such lunches in advance, after I make my routing plans for the week, has helped me bring in a number of important sales."

b. *Eliminate Backtracking And Traffic Jams.*
Strive for the most favorable routing, aiming to eliminate or minimize backtracking. The shorter the distance between calls and the less criss-crossing and backtracking you must do, the more stops you can make. At the same time, work out your travel schedules so as to avoid getting stuck in rush hour traffic jams.

The Dots and Squares Method

Phil Riordan has found more time for actual selling by working out the following routing method.

   1. He plans his travel time so as to hit the next working town in the late afternoon or evening. The first thing he does when checking into his hotel is to have the bell hop bring up a map of the city or area.

   2. He puts a dot on the map to mark the location of each customer on his list. Then he circles in red pencil the dots representing the customers with the best buying potential.

   3. Now he uses small squares to represent the location of various prospects. The best of these he outlines in blue.

   4. Starting at the point where he has the greatest concentration of red-circled dots and blue-circled squares, he connects that point with the rest of the squares and dots in such a way that he can cover every circled buyer or prospect without backtracking. This gives him a route which can be covered in minimum time while connecting with all the high-potential outlets.

5. At the same time, he connects with some of the uncircled dots and squares as fill-ins, should his prime people be unavailable.

Here is what a complete map might look like:

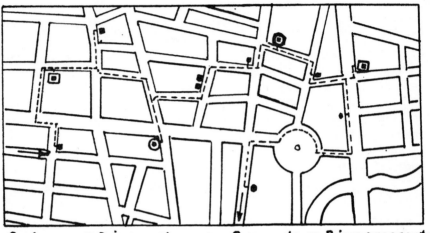

● *Customers* ◉*Prime customers* ■ *Prospects* ▣ *Prime prospects*

"I wouldn't have thought it possible before I actually tried it," Riordan reports. "But the time I gain for interviews has pushed me up into a higher earnings bracket. And although I keep moving all day, I never feel rushed."

As squares (prospects) turn into dots (customers), Riordan adds new squares. Thus he maintains a certain minimum amount of prospecting time every day.

Develop a Plans Book

Some salesmen have maximized their selling and prospecting time by working out a loose leaf Plans Book. First they set aside a page or two for each area to be visited or phoned. Then they insert these pages in their Plans Book according to the best routing as worked out above.

At the top of each page they list customers; in the bottom half, prospects. Both are graded according to the cream separating system the individual representative uses. These rankings determine, of course, the frequency of calls.

Each page is then divided by 52 down lines: one for each week. The salesman enters symbols in the appropriate place which shows why the call was made—prospecting, exploratory, final interview, servicing—and its outcome.

With a quick glance at his Plans Book, the salesman can determine if he has been calling in the proper frequency and whether his time investment on a given account has proven wise. Where changes are indicated, he can pinpoint exactly where they should be made.

Equally, on his calling days in that area, a review of the symbols alongside each customer and prospect helps the salesman plan more productive presentations.

4. PLAN FILL-IN ACTIVITIES BEFOREHAND

Some prospects or customers will always be unavailable for one reason or another. Too often this makes for unproductive time gaps only because no alternate plans were drawn up in advance.

The salesman who has prepared for such gaps can transact business with out-of-the-way customers by telephone; phone ahead for appointments; make new prospecting contacts; catch up on his paperwork or reading, etc. All it takes is an extra five or ten minutes of thought before you begin your day.

5. PUT A CEILING ON WAITING TIME

Much of your selling time is consumed in waiting to see the prospect or customer. And sometimes the waiting ends in a complete loss: you don't get to see the busy prospect anyway.

A good deal of this dead time can be slashed, and what's left of it can be put to more productive uses.

Many salesmen have found it to their advantage to limit their waiting time drastically: putting a ceiling of 30 minutes on reception room time.

Make Your Waiting Time More Productive

Whatever limits you place on it, your waiting time need *not* be *dead* time. You can conserve time in the impending interview by reviewing your presentation and arranging your material more conveniently. You can plan ahead for your next call, work on memoranda or reports, or put in some essential reading.

Many salesmen convert waiting time to exploratory time by talking to secretaries, assistants, sales people, or whoever. That way they fill out their customer file, learning more about the prospect's needs and interests.

6. MAKE MORE APPOINTMENTS

Many salesmen could squeeze more selling time out of the day by making more appointments. When you have an appointment, the customer or prospect is usually better prepared to digest your story. He may well have given thought to the impending interview before you walked in. He may ask others who can be helpful to sit in. And the chances are that his secretary will be ready to shoo you into his room as soon as you show up.

With one or two appointments set up in a neighborhood, your Plans Book will indicate other worthwhile calls which can be made, should you complete your arranged interviews faster than anticipated.

Certainly the two-interview salesman should make a strong effort to arrange a definite appointment for his follow-up calls. The one-interview salesman who uses the telephone pre-approach can reach for an appointment, too. Even when making cold calls, phoning for an appointment immediately before arriving on the scene can often lead to more productive interviews, as well as minimizing waiting time.

7. SLEEP WHERE YOU'LL WORK

When you sleep in the town you're going to be working, you can be sure of getting started the next morning with the least possible loss of time. What's more, you can often pick up valuable information on customers and prospects from the local press, hotel clerks, and other local sources.

Like New York cab drivers, small town hotel clerks amass a surprising store of information about local people—and they're not too chary about divulging it, either. With no expense and no loss of selling time, you can pick up facts that can help you land the best accounts in town.

Nor do hotel clerks exhaust the possibilities. One of the most successful salesmen of Mutual Funds, who works out of Denver, drives up to the local gas station the evening before, fills up with gas, and asks, "Who's making big money in town?"

Corny? To be sure—but it works!

And don't overlook the possibilities of the local press. Andy Bellows, who sells business insurance in a couple of southern states, makes a point of reading the local paper from stem to stern over his morning coffee. He picks up a lot of leads or good presentation ideas that way.

"Staring right at me one morning on the front page, was an account of an accident at a warehouse I was planning to call on. It seems that several men had been hurt when the 1200-pound bales they were handling toppled over. When I was paying my check, I queried the cashier and learned there had been other such accidents.

"Here was a selling point I hadn't known about. For one thing, it showed that they needed good coverage. For another, some safety measures would be helpful to them. I used that fact to establish a good rapport with the warehouse managers.

"For when I called and introduced myself, I didn't talk insurance right away. Instead, I referred to the accident I had read about and asked if they had thought of the possibilities of putting in some fork lifts. This would almost completely wipe out the safety hazard in handling those heavy bales and would cut down their insurance rates. Besides, as I pointed out, it would probably increase the speed and efficiency of their warehouse crews.

"Well, let me tell you, they were really impressed by my interest in their problems and by my knowledge of warehouse workings. What I had planned as an exploratory call, wound up in a sale."

This won't always happen when you sleep where you'll be working, but you will always save a lot of time.

IN A NUTSHELL

There's no time like now to start managing your time more effectively. To spend your time where it counts the most, work out a cream-separating system geared to your circumstances.

To add more selling time to your working day, prepare a time budget first. Then build your work-day activities around some first-things-first time-control plan, in the manner of Ivy Lee's $25,000 idea.

If you work on the outside, plan your travel and routing time on a daily or weekly basis—clustering your morning and afternoon calls around central points determined by your "must" interviews. If you sell mostly by phone, schedule your calls according to your potential rankings—and organize your desk to minimize dead time for a waiting prospect.

In either case, consider the possibilities of developing a Plans Book for easy reference to frequency of calls, conversations, and results. Where the Plans book indicates a poor investment of time, change your rankings.

Above all, remember: your selling time is your working capital.

PART II

Paving the Way for More Intangibles Sales

3

How to Use the

Customer-Oriented Pre-Approach

to Build Sales

Whenever you can, pave the way for an interview by making some kind of previous contact. For a pre-approach breaks down resistance and speeds the prospect's acceptance of your ideas.

Nor is this a matter of theory. Numerous studies have proved it out. Salesmen obtain interviews on more of their calls and close sales on more of their interviews when their visit is preceded by some earlier contact with the prospect.

Productivity Jumps

The Sales Executive's Club of New York conducted one of the more famous of these studies. Adding a pre-approach to the salesman's armory, their findings disclose, makes a salesman's calls four times more productive. Look at the actual figures:

Out of every 100 *cold* calls, salesmen received, on the average, 9.2 orders.

Out of every 100 calls made *after mail or telephone pre-approach,* salesmen received, on the average, 38.4 orders.

If anything, the pre-approach assumes even greater importance in the intangibles field than in product selling. A carload of steel, a crate of oranges, or a Fuller brush is something you can understand even if the salesman springs it on you without previous notice.

Walk in on a prospect cold with an intangible idea, and you're laboring under a handicap. For now you've got to nurse him up to the point where he can fully grasp the meaning of your proposal.

That's why a pre-approach contact, no matter how limited, gives you that jet-propelled push noted above. Because this time the prospect is with you from the very start

These are three main reasons for this jump in productivity. By analyzing each in turn, we get our first idea of what pre-approach material should contain.

1. YOU TAKE OFF THE CHILL

A pre-approach may not transform a cold suspect into a hot prospect. But it sure takes the chill off when you show up.

For years, Kenneth Caldwell has made a good thing of selling stocks and bonds through consistent pre-approach. Sometimes he uses mail, sometimes he phones.

"When I call after a mailing," he says, "I find that the man appreciates the fact that I've let him think about my visit beforehand. This puts him in a more receptive mood for my presentation.

"When I telephone first, most people are curious enough to let me tell a little of my story and this gives me an opening to suggest an appointment. If there's no interest, I feel I've saved my time for a better prospect."

Avoiding a Freeze-Out

In fact, many salesmen who work in personal sales report that home and apartment prospects have become increasingly wary of cold calls because of the talk about crime. A pre-approach contact relaxes the tension by preparing them for your call.

"I get a better reception after a mailing," notes Clark Robinson who works out of Detroit. "People are less suspicious when I identify myself as the man who sent them the letter about insurance."

2. YOU PLANT A SEED

If taking the chill off opens more doors, planting a seed opens more minds. All it means is that you incorporate an intriguing idea in your pre-approach materials that makes the recipient sit up and take notice.

If it's really something that ties in with his needs, he'll generally do some thinking about your service before you come along for the interview. Oftentimes, he may call in associates whose opinions would have a bearing on buying decisions he might make.

A Package Full of Selling

This reminds me of the time I met one of my associates headed out the door with a large package of envelopes.

"Where you headed, Hal?" I asked.

"I'm off to plant some seedlings."

"What do you mean?"

"Oh, I'm just sending out some pre-approach letters so that the seed of the idea I want people to buy will at least get a chance to sprout before I make my calls."

A Caution

Make sure you *don't* give your prospects much more than a seedling. Put too much information in your pre-approach materials and the prospect may make a negative decision before you call. And that defeats the whole purpose of the initial contact.

3. YOU MAKE MORE PRESENTATIONS

An advance letter or phone call not only warms up the atmosphere. It can considerably reduce waiting time and *wasted* time.

One national organization analyzed what happened to its salesmen when making cold calls. In more than half their calls, here's what those men told:

The prospect is in conference. He is leaving the city today. He is not in—come back this afternoon. He's out of town. He is busy. Could you come back?

The firm changed its policy. The men made more presentations.

Object: An Interview

If your pre-approach does not give you an interview, it has failed its purpose. Of course, you can no more expect that every pre-approach contact will swing an interview, than you can expect every interview to wind up with a sale. But keeping the goal firmly in mind will help step up the number of hits.

HOW TO PLAN YOUR PRE-APPROACH

In a broad sense, paving the way for the salesman refers to any kind of promotional effort that reaches the prospect prior to the salesman's call and that makes the prospect more amenable to hearing the salesman's story. But here we shall confine ourselves to the pre-approach letter or phone call whose object is an interview.

Before we go into the how-to pre-approach of letters and phone calls individually, let us first analyze some principles and techniques common to both of them.

MAKE IT LOW PRESSURE

"It's marvelous!" "It's great!" "It's the only one of its kind!"

After years of listening to shrieking superlatives, many prospects simply turn off. Sure, they're looking at you and nodding—but their mental ear plugs are tightly tamped in and you might as well have stayed home.

But they'll hear you when you drop down to a whisper. Don't offer the *best* plan; just *a* plan is good enough. You don't have the *only* program; just *a* program.

Nor do I suggest this out of a liking for becoming modesty. I am merely one of a large and growing corps who have found that low pressure in pre-approach and all selling materials sells more effectively.

Consider the following pre-approach letter that has brought in many interviews and sales because of it's calm, matter-of-fact air.

> Dear Mr. Bennett:
>
> We observe from recent Dodge reports that you are planning construction of a shopping center outside town.
>
> In the past few years we have arranged mortgage financing for several construction projects of a similar nature. We believe our experience may help us be of assistance to you.
>
> We will phone you on Monday, Sept. 15 and would appreciate a word with you then. Perhaps at that time we can arrange to get together to discuss the possibilities.
>
> We look forward to the opportunity of serving you.
>
> > Sincerely,
> >
> > Frank Emke

In the intangibles field especially, too loud an approach may cause the prospect to shy away. Absorbing an idea takes peace and quiet.

Maybe that's why this letter sells. It suggests rather than programs.

RICHARD KING BROWN ASSOCIATES
INSURANCE AND INGENUITY
FIVE THIRTY WALNUT—PHILADELPHIA 19105
TELEPHONE MAP-LIFE

July 8, 1970

Mr. Abbott P. Smith
Abbott Smith Associates, Inc.
ASA Training Consultants, Inc.
771 West End Avenue
New York, New York 10025

Dear Mr. Smith.

During the first World War there was held at the Union League a meeting participated in by Admirals, Generals and Colonels, all more or less strangers to each other.

At the end of an hour it became evident that the conference was getting nowhere. One of the men, younger than most of those present, stood it as long as he could. Finally, he mustered his courage and suggested to the august conference that military titles and the conventional order of procedure were interfering with the accomplishment of the business for which the meeting had been called. Then he made bold to suggest that in the interest of expedition they all remove their coats so that they could not see the insignia of one another's rank.

The suggestion was adopted. Coats came off; the officers became men on equal footing; ideas and arguments were considered on their merit. The meeting began to move.

I would like you, figuratively, to remove your epaulets and trade fifteen minutes of your time for fifteen minutes of mine. If at the end of fifteen minutes I have not said anything of sufficient interest to have you want me to return, I will be easy to get rid of.

When I call you by phone, you'll know that I seek an appointment to meet you.*

Sincerely yours,

RICHARD KING BROWN

RKB/rn

*©Copyright Richard King Brown of Richard King Brown Associates, 530 Walnut Street, Philadelphia, Pennsylvania.

YOUR AGENT FOR LIFE

KEEP YOUR CONTACTS VISIBLE

Sometimes a salesman who has done an excellent job of securing personalized prospect referrals from clients, "centers of influence," and the like, will fail to capitalize on these contacts in his pre-approach materials. This is equivalent to wading into a boxing ring with one hand tied behind your back.

If you prefer to operate under a self-imposed handicap, that's one thing. But if you'd really like to take advantage of every opportunity to smooth your way to an interview under the most favorable possible conditions, then make this rule number one: In every pre-approach contact—by letter or by phone—feature first and prominently any of the prospect's friends, relatives or business associates who have referred him to you.

How you can do this naturally and in low pressure fashion will be discussed in the sections on mail and telephone pre-approach.

FOLLOW THROUGH

Did you ever send out a pre-approach letter requesting that the prospect set aside a certain morning for you—and then never show up? Well, I did. It's one of the easiest ways to lose a prospect forever.

There'll be more on this later. Right now, two things need be stressed.

1. Set Up a Tickler File

A tickler file, which is common to most businesses, can be set up so as to signal to the salesman that a pre-arranged appointment is now on tap.

In setting up such a file, *do* put additional comment and qualifications on the tickler card so that you will be reminded of any important information when the man's name comes up.

If you operate on the two-interview system, a tickler file will serve double duty. For the information coupled with the reminder to prepare for the impending visit, will enable you to conduct more *successful* second interviews.

2. Send Only What You Can Follow Up

There's not much point in sending out a pre-approach letter unless you're announcing an impending visit. Broadcasting such announcements without following through is much worse.

Emil Wilder has become one of the most successful users of pre-approach materials ever since he learned that biting off more than you can chew can be fatal.

"Abbott," he once told me, "I had to learn the hard way, as so many salesmen do. You know that I generally stay a week or two in each city and town in my territory.

"Being an ambitious lug, I would send out a flock of letters to prospects in my next port of call, giving them definite dates to expect me. But again and again, I found I hadn't allowed myself half enough time to follow through."

"What happened then?"

"After a while word got round that I couldn't be depended on. That kind of thing can kill you as a salesman, so I decided I had to do something about it."

"Well, I analyzed my travel and selling time and I found that I could comfortably see five new people a day on the average. So if I allow myself a week in a particular city, I mail out 25–30 pre-approach letters at the most."

It's a simple enough formula for avoiding follow through indigestion. And it serves equally well as a preventive against over-reaching yourself when you make your pre-approach contacts by phone.

Keep Your Appointment Book Handy

One inexcusable lapse telephone pre-approachers are sometimes guilty of is doubling of appointments: arranging for two interviews at the same time—in two different places.

The solution is so obvious that it's easily overlooked: Keep your appointment book handy when you're starting your phone calls.

HOW TO PRE-APPROACH BY MAIL

With so many excellent books on letter writing available for the asking, in this section discussion shall be limited to two areas. First, I present a quick rundown of four types of pre-approach letters. Then I follow with an equally brief discussion of some basic principles conducive to good letter preparation.

FOUR TYPES OF PRE-APPROACH MAILINGS

1. Letters from the Home Office

Many companies provide their salesmen with home-office-produced mail that has but one purpose: to break the ice for the salesman. In announcing an impending visit by the salesman, such letters attempt to pave the way by planting the seed of an idea or in some way arousing the interest or curiosity of the prospect.

NO BETTER THAN THE FOLLOW-UP

Generally, the salesman has little if anything to do with the production of such home office mailings. His sole contribution—and the key one at that—is to follow through with a call *within a reasonable time* after such pieces are received.

What is a reasonable time? Here we get one of the rare cases of unanimous agreement among the experts. Unless you follow up with a visit in four days or less of time of delivery, your firm might just as well have saved its stamps.

To add insult to injury, much of this mail goes to waste *not* because the salesman fails to follow-up—but because he follows up poorly.

TIE YOUR CALL TO THE LETTER

Let's say the prospect never read the letter. Or that he tossed it into the wastebasket immediately after reading it and promptly forgot it. You can still use the existence of that letter as a peg on which to get yourself in on a favorable basis.

Here are two typical approaches, one in statement form, one posed as a question.

"Mr. Wolfram, you recently received a letter from the secretary of my company describing a plan which he believed would interest you. I am here to explain it more fully. May I have a few minutes of your time?

"Oh, you did? Well, I'm here to explain it more fully. May I have a few moments of your time?"

Or, "Oh, you didn't? Well, it will only take a few minutes of your time to explain it fully. Shall we discuss it here in your office, or would you rather do so over a cup of coffee?"

Some salesmen prefer the direct statement. Others like the flexibility of the question, and the way it draws the prospect into immediate and active interplay. Choose the one which best suits your temperament.

2. Referral Letters

Ideally, the referral letter serves as an instant ice breaker, for it brings into the very first sentence the prospect's friends, relatives or business associates acting as a reference for the salesman and his service.

The approach can be adapted to any line of intangibles, personal or business. Here, for example, is one such letter which has proven quite productive in personal sales.

> Dear Mr. Walsh:
>
> Our good customer, and your friend Marvin Westlake suggests that you would find our monthly investment plan a helpful and profitable way of building a sound portfolio.
>
> Later this week, I'll telephone you to arrange an appointment with you and Mrs. Walsh, so that I can describe this investment program in detail.
>
> I'm looking forward to meeting you both.
>
> > Sincerely,
> > Felix Walke

Note the restrained, low pressure tone. Yet Walke manages to get a quiet hint of benefits to come into this letter with those two words, "helpful and profitable."

Remember: a pre-approach letter is *not* conceived as a sales letter. It is designed purely to smooth the way for an interview.

3. Personalized Letters

That last statement holds even more true for the personalized letter. This is a pre-approach note written by you *but signed by a satisfied client who knows the recipient.*

Alternately, it can be a more broadly based letter signed by a prominent member of the community whom you know well enough to approach. This would be one of your "centers of influence."

The copy should be mild and somewhat understated, since most people would be reluctant to sign a blatant puff.

Generally, the letter will introduce you, briefly affirm that the signer has benefited in some way from the use of your service, and then suggest that the recipient might benefit in the same manner. Here is an example: typically short and direct.

> "David Morgan recently provided service for me that has saved me a considerable amount of time and money. As this service was of value to me, I thought it possibly might be of some value to you.
>
> "David tells me he will phone you for an appointment within a few days."

Sincerely,

Actually, the original letter ended with the first paragraph, perpetuating an error that many pre-approach writers endlessly repeat. That is, they make no reference to a planned visit or to a telephone call to arrange an appointment.

True, the pre-approach is not a sales contact in reference to your service itself. *But it is selling an* appointment—*and like sales of any kind, it should ask for the order.*

HOW PROMINENT IS YOUR CHIEF EXECUTIVE

In the case of a bank, a letter signed by the president who was well known for his involvement in civic affairs, turned out to be a good, personalized pre-approach for the bank's contact officers. It successfully paved the way for calls promoting Check-Credit lines to the top business executives of that community.

If *your* boss is prominent enough, why not suggest appending his signature to a "center of influence" letter?

4. "Do-It-Yourself" Letters

The personalized letter quoted above also falls into the "do-it-yourself" category. But here I want to stress the friendly and informal mailings that can go out from your own office, over your own signature.

In this connection, a few simple rules will help you draw up pre-approach letters that will do the job they're supposed to do. Basically, a good pre-approach letter should answer three questions the recipient will normally raise in his own mind:

    1. What is it?

2. Why should I read it?

3. What does he want me to do?

Here, for example, is a short, simple letter that answers all three questions directly and with no wasted motion.

> Dear Dr. Gerbi:
>
> My company has designed an unusual savings and investment plan that has been of great interest to other men in the medical profession. *(What it is)* Your colleague, Dr. Helene Holtz, says that the half hour she reserved for me last week was time well spent."

(Why he should read: his colleague recommends it; it is "time well spent.")

> "If we could spend a half hour together sometime in the afternoon of Wednesday, March 18, you can then determine whether or not this plan might be of value to you, too."

(What he should do)

> "I will phone on Tuesday to check the exact appointment time."
>
> > Sincerely,
> > George Ackerman

The *"what-is-it?"* poses few difficulties—apart from the need for compression. It is merely a description of your service, quickly and succinctly stated.

The *"why-should-I-read-this?"* is a bit more complex. Not, however, because it is difficult but because it offers more possibilities.

Always it should be no more than a brief, tantalizing hint of interesting or useful possibilities. This reason to read can be presented as a seed planting idea; a whiff of a benefit to be gained; a hint of problems that can be solved. Where you have a referral contact on tap, name him and let him plant the seed.

A Post-Card Pre-Approach

Here is an interesting case where the referral was the salesman's "nest" rather than a specific individual. Alfred Gibbs does "nest" prospecting at several large industrial plants in Southern California. He sells over a million dollars worth of insurance each year with the help of this simple, informal post-card pre-approach.

> Dear Mr. Crandall:
>
> "I've been exchanging valuable ideas on estate insurance *(What it is)* with many of the engineers at your company. While I haven't had the opportunity of meeting you yet, you have been recommended to me as a man who might find this service advantageous.

(Why he should read—and listen)

> "Would coffee on Tuesday or lunch on Thursday be better

for you to see me? I will phone on Monday to find out which
day is more convenient."
(What the sender wants him to do: choose a lunch or coffee date.)

Tell Them You'll Be Calling

This is the final—but no less important—rule. *Don't* sign off without
letting the prospect know that you'll be dropping in for an interview. In
all of the examples given, the salesman also announced that he would be
phoning to confirm the suggested appointment.

This makes such a powerful follow-up device that I could well present
it as a basic rule, too. Now along comes Robert Wilhelm, another post-card
pre-approacher who mails out two-sentence messages telling his prospects
the exact day he will call.

But Wilhelm makes no follow up phone call. Says he: "I give them no
chance to turn me down."

And his post-card contact balances on the edge of the other rule vio-
lations. All of which shows that exceptions to rules are fine—so long as
they work!

His message: "I'm planning to call on you next Tuesday morning to
discuss with you some new ideas in direct mail advertising. These productive ideas are based on a study of what the most progressive whole-
salers in this country have been doing along these lines."

HOW TO PRE-APPROACH BY TELEPHONE—AND GET THE INTERVIEW

In Chapter 14, *How To Use Sales Tools,* we analyze in depth the technique of persuasive telephone usage. In this section, we shall briefly touch
upon the *content* of the telephone pre-approach. Briefly, only because
much of what was discussed under mail pre-approach also applies to telephone contacts.

All the ingredients of a good telephone pre-approach can be squeezed
into a very brief conversation. Here is a typical example:

"Mr. Driscoll, this is Anton Thurston of Intercontinental Express. Recently we worked out a shipment schedule for Bill
Henley over at Mainline Fabrics that helped him sew up an important contract. Bill was so pleased with the way we handled
the problem that he suggested I get in touch with you.

"I wonder if we could meet on Monday, or would the latter
part of the week be better for you?"

Three Steps to Effective Telephone Pre-Approach

Brief though it was, you will find when you analyze it that Thurston's
call adhered to the same basic points underlying a sound letter pre-approach.

1. Identify yourself and your firm.
2. Give the prospect a reason for listening—and peg the reason to a personal referral, when possible.
3. Ask for an appointment.

Let us expand a bit upon the last two.

GIVE THE PROSPECT A REASON FOR LISTENING

Most people who pick up the phone only to hear a salesman at the other end, have a natural impulse to slam the receiver down again. There's only one way you can stop them: Give them a good reason for listening— and do it fast.

Self-interest, curiosity and mutual friends or associates are among the more powerful inducers. Use any of them and you'll arrest the receiver in it's cut-off flight. Use all of them and you'll have your prospect with you all the way.

But the need for speed argues a parallel need for preparation. *Don't* trust to off-the-cuff inspiration. *Do* plan what you will say before you make your pre-approach contact.

While the examples in this section have differences corresponding to the differing temperaments of the salesmen cited, they *all* have two vital factors in common. They observe the three pre-approach steps; they were planned in advance.

Personal Referral

A personal referral is perhaps the easiest way to hold the prospect. Ted Baker gets the name in even before he identifies his firm.

"Mr. Hammil, this is Ted Baker, a friend of Charles Kingston. I am with the Tri-State Insurance Company and I recently helped Charlie rearrange his insurance and estate program.

"Charlie thought it would be a good idea if I spoke to you along the same lines. He told me to tell you that he was amazed at how much we extended his present coverage by using certain settlement options and an insurance trust.

"I'd like to meet you to see if this service might be of interest to you. Which would be better for you, morning or afternoon?"

Mind you, this entire message takes less than a minute on the phone. And Ted packs "reasons for listening" into every second!

1. He identifies himself immediately as a friend of a friend.
2. He implies how useful he might be to the prospect in the same sentence that identifies his firm.
3. He lets friend Charlie enthuse about the beneficial impact of Ted's expertise. And he arouses curiosity about "certain settlement options."
4. Finally, he gives a reason for listening to an interview: "to see if this service might be of interest to you."

Generalized Referral

What if you have no friend or business associate to refer to? You can generalize. You can cite other men *in similar circumstances;* companies *in similar businesses;* or institutions *with similar needs.*

To illustrate the point, consider how another insurance salesman has used a cold-call approach to catapult himself onto the Million Dollar Round Table.

"Mr. Lamston, this is Pete Ellenburg with Southern State Insurance. Have you a moment to speak on the phone?

"Good. Mr. Lamston, I have no way of knowing if you're interested in the purchase of life insurance at this time. *However, I have a service that has made it possible for other men in your position to increase their benefits without any additional cost to them.*" And he goes on to his close.

Ignorance and Curiosity

A friend of mine sells mortgages to private investors, many of whom have never bought discounted mortages before and have only the haziest notion of what they might be. To educate them on the phone would be fatal. It would distract from the main purpose of the pre-approach: getting an interview. And it would arouse resistance before Al could get around to handling it.

What's left? A straightforward appeal to self-interest and curiosity. Here's how he does it.

"Mr. Jarret, we have a plan which many men in situations like yours are using to fill out the security side of their investment portfolios. May I come to your office to tell you about it?"

Venerable, perhaps, but it works. It's so simple and direct, so free of exaggeration or pressure, that it's hard to refuse.

Pre-Approaching a Suspect

When making a telephone pre-approach to an unqualified contact, you follow the same three pre-approach rules. But you preface your message with a qualifying query. Like this:

"Mr. Woodridge, this is Nat Stewart of the Empire Financing Company. You and I haven't met, but Frank Heilman, one of your good suppliers, tells me you were planning to expand your business within the next few months. Is that correct?"

(Qualifying the need.)

"Yes, it is."

(Stewart immediately sweeps into his pre-approach.)

"I'm glad to hear that. Frank didn't say anything about your plans or your financial situation, but we find that most men who plan a major expansion find themselves in need of some kind of financing. My firm has been able to help Frank and many other businessmen in this area expand their businesses without worry over money."

In one brief call, he has qualified a new prospect and has carried him to the point where he can ask for the interview.

ASK FOR THE APPOINTMENT

As always, no sales contact is worthy of the name unless you close it actively. But remember: People will respond more readily when you give them a choice.

"Would the morning or the afternoon be better for you?" "Which is more convenient for you, your home or your office?" "Would lunch today or Friday be better for you?"

Handling Objectives

Since all you're asking for is an appointment, most objections fall into one or another "evasive action" category. Typical answers to the three most typical objections follow.

"Can't you tell me over the phone?"

"I'm sorry, Mr. Young. For me to attempt to discuss this over the phone would hardly do justice to your needs. It will take less than 30 minutes for me to show you how this idea can save time and money for you. Would the morning or afternoon be more convenient for you?"

(When the prospect is resisting an appointment, it makes sense to minimize the time involved—if you truly can.)

"Can't you send it to me in the mail?"

"I'll be glad to, Mr. Quentin. However, I must get some information from you first in order to send you a plan designed to meet your needs. Would you be available Wednesday afternoon, or would Thursday be better?"

"It sounds like a good idea, but I can't do anything now."

"*When* you act on this plan is entirely up to you, Mr. Vinson. All I want to do is show you *how* this idea can help you and your family. When is the best time to get together with you and Mrs. Vinson, the middle of the week, or the weekend?"

(Again, this salesman doesn't argue the point. He just stresses the benefits —then tries again.)

COORDINATED PRE-APPROACH

Used separately as pre-approach tools both the mails and the telephone produce good results. But they undoubtedly are most effective when combined into a coordinated attack.

Proof of the Pudding

For a long time, one Chicago firm sent out 1,000 pre-approach letters a week for each of its salesmen—with very poor results. Finally, management engaged a consultant to improve its direct mail techniques.

His recommendation: send out only 100 letters per man—but follow up with telephone calls to press for appointments.

The salesmen objected. "How can we get enough good leads from 100 letters," they wanted to know, "if we don't get enough from 1,000?"

Ultimately the men were persuaded—on the basis of previous experience —to give the plan a try. Here's what was done:

1. Each salesman mailed 100 letters: 50 on one day, another 50 on the next.
2. Seventy-two hours after the first batch of letters went out, each salesman phoned his first 50 prospects and tried for appointments. Ditto for the second batch one day later.
3. On each call, the salesman referred to the letter immediately, after identifying himself and his firm.

Results? Uniformly, those salesmen made more appointments and closed more sales from the 100-letters-and-phone-calls combination than they had ever reached with the 1,000 letter mailings.

Nor was that all. By the third week, the most experienced salesmen had tapered off to 75 letters a week. For they could no longer handle the number of appointments they were getting from the letter mailings.

Three Rules

When using the letter-phone call pre-approach, three rules must be added to those discussed above: one on timing; one on letter content; one on telephone call.

1. In closing the letter, let the prospect know you will phone to confirm an appointment.
2. Phone the prospect no more than 24 hours after he *receives* your pre-approach letter. (This of course, is the equivalent of the 72-hour *after* mailing follow up.)

Tests have shown that the recipient's memory of and interest in the pre-approach letter is retained on the average for just one day. After that, both memory and interest plummet to the vanishing point.

3. Refer to the letter immediately after identifying yourself and your firm.

Nobody knows quite why, but whatever the reason, immediate reference to the letter whets the prospect's interest in your telephone follow-up —provided you haven't exceeded the 24-hour limit. Even when the prospect hasn't read the letter, mention of it serves to arouse his curiosity.

One example will suffice to illustrate the pattern of the follow-up call.

"Good morning, Mr. Callahan. This is George Brockton with Mutual of Omaha. I wonder if you received the letter I sent you several days ago?"

"You did? Then you know that I'm calling to find out if you have a plan that pays you a regular monthly income when you're sick or hurt and can't work."

(Qualifying the prospect before moving on to the pre-approach proper.)

"I see. Well, in that case you'd probably like to learn more about our plan which pays lifetime benefits for either accident or sickness. Would Wednesday or Thursday evening be more convenient for you?"

A Unique 3-Way Combination

One business systems salesman in Minneapolis has built a respectable volume with a 3-way combination of his own devising.

1. He mails out a pre-approach letter.

2. That very *same* day he phones to identify himself and inform the prospect that he will receive a letter the next day which he is sure will be of interest. And he winds up as follows:

"After you've received this letter, discussed it with your associates and, perhaps, with your accountant; I will call again for an appointment."

Brash? Perhaps.

But his success argues that this pre-approach to the pre-approach letter makes the prospect actually look forward to a letter that would otherwise be processed in routine fashion.

3. Two days later he makes his follow-up call. This intensive pre-approach cultivation nets him a high percentage of interviews—and sales.

CAPSULE SUMMARY

Your pre-approach contact—whether by mail, telephone or both—has one primary objective: to open the door to an interview.

But in achieving this end, three corollary goals will generally be secured as well.

1. You take the chill off the impending interview—thus insuring a more responsive welcome to your presentation.

2. You make your prospect do some thinking about your proposition *before* you call. This will help you retain his interest as you go more deeply into your story.

3. You give him a strong intimation of benefits to come. This serves as the first plank in your closing foundation.

The three golden rules of pre-approach: Give your prospects a reason for listening (or reading). Give them a reason for granting an interview. Then ask them for one.

Even if you don't work for a concern that provides you with direct mail materials, you can organize a do-it-yourself pre-approach campaign by following the step-by-step rules outlined in this chapter and by adapting some of the examples to your own needs. In some cases, it might be worthwhile going to a pro in the field, such as an ad agency specializing in direct mail.

4

How to Prepare
More Constructive Sales Calls

Once upon a time, a salesman could rely upon a quick tongue and a persuasive personality to produce sales volume. For better or worse, that day has long since passed.

Today, orders and profits turn directly on the degree of constructive thought a salesman can bring to bear upon any given situation. For every sale reflects the buyer's conviction that your service will help him solve or ease one of his special headaches. As a Purchasing Agent for General Electric sums it up: "We like to see the salesman who can show how his product or service will help us out on specific problems.

That one phrase underscores the entire rationale for creative selling. For the creative sell has two interlinked facets:

1. You place the prospect's problems in the center of the stage.
2. With his attention thus secured, you lead him into consideration of your services, shaping your presentation to fit *his* needs as *he* sees them.

Creative Selling Means Giving

One successful salesman of business insurance puts it this way: "Selling begins and ends with giving: giving our time and skills in defining and solving the customer's problems, or in our thoughtfulness in offering useful ideas. The biggest rewards go to the salesman who gives the most; not in the service he sells—but in the widest variety of well-chosen 'helps.' "

Giving Can Be Small

Nor need it be elaborate. Indeed, you will not find it easy in most cases to come up with something dramatic. But where competing salesmen offer essentially the same services at the same price, just a small creative touch can turn the trick.

Consider a case in point. Recently, a management consultant asked two printers to quote prices on an offset job for 500,000 small booklets with a large number of dealers' imprints. Both outfits sent samples of their work plus all the information requested. Each did equally fine work and their prices were not far apart.

But one printer had gone to the trouble of checking on how the booklets were to be used. (Placing the prospect's problem in the center of the stage.)

With this information under his belt that creative printer made it easy for the consulting firm to grasp his quotations. He organized them in such a manner that the principals could take in almost at a glance the breakdowns required for resale to each customer.

The other firm gave the overall price alone. It took more than an hour to translate its figures into the form needed to quote resale prices.

Obviously, the constructive extra provided by the first firm tipped the balance in its direction. And the first order was hardly the last.

That's the way of it. A creative approach* builds a favored position for the immediate sale; at the same time, it lays the foundations for a lasting relationship.

Supply and Demand

Most salesmen agree that finding out about the prospect's problems and doing something about them will open up doors to extra sales and earnings. But agree or not, the real question is: How often do you do it?

Researchers have asked hundreds of buyers on whom salesmen call regularly: "What percentage of salesmen come in with a plan to be helpful, something that demonstrates a constructive interest in your needs?"

According to these experienced buyers, less than half the salesmen who call regularly come in with such plans or intentions. As one man commented sourly: "Sales pitches are commonplace, but it's rare to find a genuine interest in our problems."

Opportunities Galore

Now consider the reverse side of the coin. If most salesmen do *not* rate as well as they should from the buyers' viewpoint, then think of the opportunities opened up to those who correct this deficiency. Such opportunities present themselves to every seller of intangibles.

*By "creative approach" I mean the entire job of digging out problems; working out solutions; shaping a presentation around them. "Constructive call" I confine to the selling interview alone—one built around solutions or helpful ideas slanted toward the prospect's interests.

"Let's Make Sure We Understand the Problem"

An insurance salesman who has built an impressive personal following, invariably opens on this creative note: "Before we talk about policies, let's make sure we understand the problem." Diving headlong into the area of his prospect's own interests, he captures immediate attention.

Should the prospect start questioning him about a specific policy too early on, this salesman will say: "Before I answer, I want to know what *your* special problems are."

Then he counters with his own queries.

This makes it all the more impressive when he finally presents his case. For by that time the prospect is literally on edge for the thoughtful suggestions he now *expects* to hear.

No wonder this creative salesman closes an average of six sales for every 10 qualified prospects he calls on.

Building Lasting Relationships

Or take the securities field. The hit-and-run salesman will push whatever he feels will move fastest and earn the most *now*.

The creative seller is also out for a sale—but he keeps one eye peeled for the future. He knows there are all kinds of customers, just as there are all kinds of securities. His job as he sees it is to make the proper match, the one that reconciles his own interests with those of his prospect's.

Merrill, Lynch, Pierce, Fenner and Smith has marched to its preeminent position on the heels of one cardinal rule. As a Senior Vice President recently defined it: "Our sales rest *not* on whether we can make money in a given situation—but on whether it is to our customer's advantage."

Hit and run sales for immediate gain can build volume and earnings in the short run. But in the end, they hurt you, your customers, and your industry.

In this age of intensified competition and growing resistance to the "hard sell," the successful salesman is the one who can originate more creative approaches to his prospects and customers. To score more creative sales, center your thoughts on two basic areas:

1. Get close to the prospect's problems.
2. Prepare a constructive call.

I. GET CLOSE TO THE PROSPECT'S PROBLEMS

At the meeting which marks the end of each training session for new salesmen, one sales manager closes the proceedings with these final comments:

"We must assume that the most worthwhile customers and prospects upon whom we call are currently being solicited by our competition. They have heard all the standard 'sales approaches'; so if we merely duplicate the call methods our competitors use, our lack of imagination will leave no hinge upon which to base a reasoned decision in our favor. The prospect might just as well toss a coin.

"To gain a competitive advantage, we have to use constructive imagination, gearing our approaches to the solution of prospect and customer problems."

Then he sums up succinctly: "No problem, no sale."

Once you start looking for them you'll find plenty of problems—and plenty of sales on the strength of them. For your firm's services will help ease many a prospect headache if only you knew they existed.

Before you can help him, then, you've got to bring his problems into the open. How do you do that? Basically, in two ways.

1. Investigate before you call.
2. Explore the situation when you call.

A. INVESTIGATE BEFORE YOU CALL

The groundwork for any sale can be laid before you walk in the door. And the more information you gather beforehand, the better your chances of making a telling presentation. Nor is this a matter of theory.

What the Buyers Say

In the survey quoted above, buyers were also queried on that which *they* regarded as good or bad selling. It is instructive to see how many resent the salesman who walks in on them *with no prior knowledge* of their needs.

Take this typical comment: "I am constantly amazed that so many salesmen know so little about our specific needs and problems. They want us to buy—but they don't even take the trouble to find out how their services might be of value to us."

Note the phrase: ". . . they don't even take the trouble . . . ." It cropped up again and again—revealing a deep-seated resentment of salesmen who don't consider the customer's needs important enough to study beforehand.

"As I see it," one buyer writes bluntly, "if the salesman wants an order he ought to take the trouble to find out what I want and help me get it."

Look Before You Leap

There you have it. Digging out problems via a preliminary study helps you peg the interview to issues of immediate interest to the prospect. At times it helps you call with a prepared solution.

Obviously, this puts you on the inside track—even where the problem or solution does not tie in directly to your services.

For example, when qualifying a large-scale dealer in the building materials field, one salesman found that the prospect could use his services but wasn't sure "we could afford the investment at this time." The salesman arranged an interview regardless, but decided that further investigation was warranted beforehand.

As it happened, the prospect banked in the same institution that serviced the salesman's firm. A discreet check of this obvious source of information disclosed that the prospect had a flourishing business but was plagued by a serious cash-flow problem traceable to his unusually high inventories.

Now the salesman's investigation turned to contacts in the prospect's line of business. "Why those high inventories?" he wanted to know.

The answer was simple and typical enough. The prospect's biggest customers were building contractors working on big residential or business construction complexes. They ordered materials by the carload—and they wanted them on the construction sites when they needed them. Hence the inventories.

Now let the salesman take it from there. "The fact that I learned about this problem before I called helped me come in with an idea that made me the original fair-haired boy as far as this prospect was concerned. For I suggested that he consolidate his buying with one or two of his biggest suppliers, concerns that could guarantee delivery within a few days of each contractor's on-the-site requirements. This made it unnecessary for the prospect to continue to tie up his operating capital in huge inventories.

"My own service? He bought without bothering to check out competitive offers."

The Question of Time

True, the extent and depth of a preliminary investigation must conform to the economics of the situation and to the type of service you sell. Yet often enough, all it takes to gain a competitive advantage is the habit of scanning newspapers and professional literature for professional information, as Larry Nash does.

Taking Time to Read

Larry, who sells accounting services, beefed up his first call in typical (for Larry) fashion. That is, he dropped an important piece of news into a brief introductory remark.

"Mr. Karp, I dropped by today just to tell you about a state law which was passed this morning. Wherever you do your banking, you should open a separate Insurance Premium checking account."

At this, the broker perked up his ears. "What's it all about? I haven't had time to read the papers today."

"I know how it is, "Larry said sympathetically. "But keeping up with such things is part of my business." (A neat selling touch.)

Then he went on to explain the law more thoroughly and how an Insurance Premium account would protect the broker's interests. And he walked out with an appointment to discuss his own services in two days' time. Once again, a creative approach paved the way to a sale.

Of Time and Recurring Situations

When you can do the job briefly enough, you'll rarely question the value of a preliminary study. Equally, a big sale or a long-range profit potential will justify the time and effort put into wide-ranging investigation.

But the thoughtful salesman will consider the investment of investigating time on low-ticket sales—when he sees the possibility of adapting the findings to recurring situations. An example will make this clear.

Kenneth Dutton has become one of the top performers for a firm selling service to department stores. Despite competitive pressures, the low profit per unit sale made extensive pre-call study apparently unjustified.

But early in his career Dutton found the same set of problems cropping up in one store after another: problems his service was designed to ease. On his own initiative, he took a step previously unheard of in his field. Devoting two weeks to study these problems, *he worked out general solutions which could be quickly modified to fit the slight variations from prospect to prospect.*

Ever since, in the first 15 minutes of his presentation he focuses exclusively on the need for his service—backing up each statement with factual evidence from his study. Then he talks solutions. And now he has a file of customer records and trade paper clippings testifying to the favorable effect of his services upon department store sales.

Know What You're Looking For

Speaking of recurring situations, you can control the time you devote to preliminary investigation when you know in which direction to look. A real estate broker, for example, knows that his prospects will often worry about down payments. So he'll automatically look into the situation and check out sources of credit, if needed.

Finding the Right Service

Similarly, a bank officer knows that a prospect will often ask for a service which does *not* best suit the prospect's needs. This immediately defines an area of investigation which can win a new account or preserve an old one.

Take the banker who called upon a partnership which had asked for a line of credit of $10,000. This business had been formed by two partners pooling practically all of their personal assets.

Although they had met with reasonable success, the banker could see they were not yet in a position to borrow on this basis. Besides, he felt they needed additional temporary working capital, not interim credit.

When he called, he was prepared to show them exactly why a Small Business Loan was the right service for them. As he pointed out:

"1. The business really needed more temporary working capital. About $7,000 would do the trick.

2. The partnership could more easily afford the small monthly payback.

3. The life of the older partner, who owned a 75% interest, would be insured for the life of the loan."

As this officer reports: "I really didn't have much selling to do. Presenting the right service for them was such a constructive step in itself that it did the job for me."

Problems to Look For: A Checklist

Given a general checklist, augmented by the more specific items you can add out of your own experience, you can narrow the range of preliminary study from prospect to prospect. And remember, you can gain a favored position by exposing and solving problems whether or not they relate to your services.

1. When selling to business, you might address yourself to these problems:

Are his production costs too high? Is he seriously limited in space? Is his inventory too big or too small? What kind of customers does he have? Are his employees disgruntled because of pension or health insurance plans? Has a high accident rate affected his insurance costs?

2. When selling personal services:

Is he a home owner? Does he need financing for repairs? How many children does he have? Are they pre-school or college age? Is there chronic illness in the family? Is he approaching retirement? Is he self-employed? Does he have extra sources of income? Many others you can develop.

Which of these checklist items suggest themselves as avenues for preliminary study will rest on what you sell in general, and to whom you sell in each given case. But the more you add to these lists and the more you consult them, the more quickly you can pave the way to an approach the *buyers* want.

Know Your Sources

You know what you need to look for. But the question is: how do you go about finding it?

Some of the answers to that question are scattered throughout this book. Many others are obvious.

If you're on the personal sales side, you'll root around the prospect's neighborhood. For neighbors and local tradesmen are all grist to your mill.

If you're selling to business, you can often use others in the same or related industries; suppliers, trade papers, credit rating agencies, banks, or your own company's files quickly present themselves as sources of pre-call information.

In short, most any salesman can get the facts when he puts his mind to it. The trick is to build the habit of thinking about sources of information which can turn up the one vital fact your competitors may overlook. Two examples will show the value of such thinking when high potential sales are involved.

Library Research

Haunting the library stacks may not generally fall under the heading of hustling for business. But my friend John Mullins won an extremely lucrative and long lasting account because of a research job worthy of the most dedicated academic.

John sells services for a major publishing house. One day, as he tells it, he heard that a factoring concern in the cotton industry—one of the largest outfits in the business—was in the market for the kind of financial services John handles.

But he knew nothing about factoring. Nor could he hope to make a sale of that nature if he made his initial call without plenty of factual information to backstop any discussion of plans.

In those days, factors did not exactly advertise for business, so there were no promotional pieces to help him. Pondering the problem of information sources, John suddenly thought, "That's what libraries are for."

Whereupon he spent hours in the central reference room of the public library reading books on the subject. Factors, he discovered, provide operating capital for industries that process goods, but whose capital requirements are so great that they cannot keep a steady flow of goods without turning to outside sources for operating money.

Then John spent more hours making notes on information that applied particularly to factoring for the textile industry.

Finally he was ready for an interview with the head of the firm.

"When I phoned for an interview, my new-found ability to talk the language of the factoring business helped me set up an appointment for the next day.

"That night I reviewed all my notes on the possible application of our services to his business, with special emphasis on some of the problems we could help ease."

"And did he buy?" I asked.

"He bought all right, and it was one of the shortest presentations I ever had to make. But that isn't all. He offered me a job! He told me that very few of his own men knew as much about the factoring business even after their first few months in the field as I did."

Lunch for a Lowly Bookkeeper

Business equipment and systems is an extremely competitive field with large sales riding on every interview. The man who does the best job of preparing himself for the initial call, has the best chance to get the business.

"You can't get anywhere in this field," says salesman Gerald Crosby, "unless you pick up a load of background facts before you call. Many of us will entertain executives from the prospect's firm or elsewhere as part of our fact finding ritual. But I find that very often I can come up with useful information by taking a lower level employee to lunch."

Once, for example, he scouted an important prospect for a week before he made his call. By chatting with one of the bookkeepers at lunch, he discovered the accounting department was working overtime all that week.

Digging deeper, he found that this happened almost every month because of the type of calculating machines that the firm used. "That was all the clue I needed to plan my approach," Gerald remarked.

"When I finally called on the prospect, I had a plan based on *his* problem and backed by actual figures. For our plan had saved six firms in his industry up to $300 a month in labor costs alone by drastically reducing the amount of overtime needed."

With one more call, after getting some additional information the prospect wanted, Gerald started a new account.

One Interview—or Two

As our examples have indicated, a pre-call investigation will open the door to extra sales in both the one-and two-interview systems.

In one sense, the one-interview man needs it most. For he walks in to close the sale in one fell swoop. The more facts he picks up beforehand, the more readily he can lead his prospect to the dotted line.

For the two-interview man, a preliminary study serves to narrow down the area of his fact-finding call. Thus, the more surely he will dig out the information essential to a productive selling presentation.

Two interviews or one, all prospects are different; a creative presentation must still be tailored to individual circumstances. No matter how you do it, you'll take a long step toward your sale when you gather information *before* you call.

And you'll get much closer when you explore the situation face-to-face.

B. EXPLORE WHEN YOU CALL

In many intangibles fields, the exploratory call is a necessity. Salesmen selling group insurance, for example, wouldn't get very far without a fact-finding interview to back up their preliminary study.

Necessity or not, exploring the situation boils down to two words we've conjured with before: *Observe* and *inquire.* Since observations generally determine the direction of your queries, let's start there.

1. Get In and Watch

Down in Panama City, Florida, Dave Robertson, head of the Dave Robertson Electric Company, sells many contracting jobs that call for more work and more money than the customer intended to spend.

As Mr. Robertson puts it: "I sell 'future expansion' in every commercial installation."

How does he do it?

According to *Electrical South,* the entire secret lies in the way he builds his proposals on the sound foundation of facts uncovered by observation. Walking through plant and office, and dropping adroit questions in his wake, Robertson pieces together a full picture of his prospect's present business, his future outlook, his needs and his hopes. "I find out what services are needed for immediate operation and for the next two years' increase in business—and then double that amount."

By doing this, to take one example out of many, he sold an 800 ampere circuit to an ice plant whose owners had planned on 400 amperes. That plant now has easy, inexpensive access to capacity for 10 years of expansion—and has already dipped into its reserve power.

While they had signed the contract a shade hesitantly, the company executives now brag about their foresight. What's more, they steer new customers to Dave Robertson Electric.

"I take the trouble to find out their plans *and* their dreams for the future, then I show them how I can help those dreams materialize," Dave Robertson sums it up.

He Rides the Cars First

Any prospect will be pleased to know that you're interested enough in him to take that kind of trouble. That's why National Cash Register trains its salesmen never to talk business with a prospect before he allows them to study his particular situation.

Oscar Chubb finds that the same technique pays off for him. His firm sells a full maintenance package that keeps elevators running after years of rugged service.

When Oscar first looks in on his prospect, he doesn't try to sell him—

yet. "I don't want to talk business until I know more about your requirements," he says.

Instead, he asks to ride the elevators to study operating efficiency; the response to floor controls, rise and descent times, and other factors. He also arranges to look over the engine room.

This done, he returns to the prospect's office. There he looks into the number and length of shutdowns, the cost of repairs, the interference with other building operations and the like. When he calls back to talk business, he has "a tailor-made plan that will eliminate unnecessary shutdowns and expense."

At this point, Oscar has psychology going for him. For his on-the-job study has already created a favorable mental set: his prospect *expects* an individualized service deal that will solve his problems.

The One-Interview Salesman

The case of Oscar Chubb raises a quite important point. For just as he adapted the National Cash Register approach to his own needs, so the one-interview salesman can bend the exploratory call to the requirements of the one-interview system.

How?

All you need do is split your call into two halves. In the first half you observe, inquire, talk needs and problems. In the second half—with your prospect primed to hear what you can do for *him*—you present your plan, and close.

When securities salesman Charles Merril tells a prospect, "Let's see if you should aim primarily for 'go-go' returns or secure income," he's "watching the operation" in terms of a personal, one-interview sale. When he starts to close, he's conducting his "second interview"—all in the one visit.

Surveys and Recurring Situations

Many individuals have had a life insurance salesman offer to survey their insurance needs and existing coverage. (Another one-interview "operation-watching" approach.) This creative approach to sales could be used much more often in other fields—and with beneficial results for all concerned.

In this case, the customer was unaware that he had a problem until the salesman's on-the-spot study pinpointed the need for a balanced inventory. As so often happens, uncovering the problems closed the sale almost of itself.

"A basic and recurring problem for me," writes Gilbert Snow of the ABC Financing Company, "is to convince my prospects that they need the investment capital we can supply. For example, the owner of a large retail shoe store chain was sure he had no business problem which called for additional investment. Yet my preliminary inquiry convinced me otherwise.

"To tell him he was wrong point blank would be fatal. Instead, after some discussion, I received his permission to make a study of no-sale walkouts at his biggest store on Friday night and Saturday, their peak selling days. This study disclosed that 27% walked out because they could not be fitted properly, and 17% because they couldn't find a particular style in stock.

"When my prospect saw these figures and grasped their significance, he immediately became receptive to the idea of stocking a broader range of sizes in the basic styles which accounted for most of his sales, as well as the need to widen his inventory of styles. Instead of tying up his capital for such purchases, we would finance them.

"I made the sale. But more important, *I was able to use this study to convince a number of other dealers that they too could increase their business appreciably by carrying an in-depth inventory*—which we could finance on competitive terms."

As the *italicized* portion indicates, once you work out a good creative attack on a problem, you can often apply it to a number of other prospects.

With your preliminary exploration coupled to on-the-spot observation, you have a pretty good idea of the prospect's personal or business problems. Now you're ready to complete the job.

2. Inquire Consistently

Most people appreciate the chance to talk about their problems with a sympathetic listener, particularly one who might help. By the same token, they'll resist the salesman who displays little interest in probing their needs. Indeed, inquiry is so important to the intangibles salesman that I am almost tempted to say: "inquire even if you've previously acquired all the information you need."

If nothing else, it would be a soft sell way of letting the facts emerge.

One Man Asked

Take a case in point. A trustee of the biggest hospital in town, an intimate of many of its leading doctors, bought a good, centrally located drugstore. When word got around that he was building a second one, many suppliers called on him, including representatives of three wholesale drug houses.

Two stressed the importance of stocking a balanced line of drugs and sundries. Each got a small order.

The third man *asked* the prospect: "What are your own ideas for these stores?"

Said the owner, "I want to work in drugs, not a department store. I want a place that doctors will like and that people will think of when they have prescriptions to fill."

Now that he knew what was on his prospect's mind, the salesman went all out on the one theme; his house as a provider of pharmaceutical services. He stressed their detailing of pharmacists on new prescription items and dosage forms, the maintenance of an Rx information service for their customers, their new motorcycle fleet for emergency deliveries, the occasional seminars they organized on new drugs, and the maintenance inventory keyed to the special items required by leading local physicians.

This firm became the druggist's chief supplier, even though the man who headed one of the competing outfits was a good friend. Some time later, this friend asked: "Why have you given most of your business to my competitor?"

In answer, the druggist described the services his supplier offered. "But we could do the same," his friend remarked.

"Maybe so," the owner said. "But your representative never asked me about my interests. Their's did."

And mind you, all he did was ask one question!—"What are your *own* ideas for these stores?"

It's Never Too Late

If there is one topic a man likes to discuss, it is himself and his business. One question or five, exploratory inquiry displays your interest in the prospect, focuses the interview on his problems and needs, lets you tie your plan directly to them.

And it's never too late. The man who says "no" to a regular call, may well be open to a creative sell.

Harvey Halliday, who handles oil heating systems sold mainly to householders, tells of one such instance. One day his territory was expanded to an area that included an 11-unit greenhouse smack in the middle of a residential neighborhood.

But when he tried to make a sale, he was turned down. "Soft coal is cheaper and more efficient for the huge boilers we use," the prospect explained. And he wouldn't be budged.

As Halliday made his rounds in this new territory, he found the residents up in arms against the black smoke continually belching out of the greenhouse chimneys. There was a lot of talk about changing the zoning laws and forcing the greenhouse to move.

That gave Halliday his cue. Back he marched to the greenhouse, opening this time with the question that placed the key problem out in front where it belonged.

"Do you know about the campaign for new zoning laws, aimed at your plant?"

"We sure do and I admit it has us worried."

"Then tell me, *why* do you need such tremendous boilers?"

(This could be in Halliday's normal selling armory. When tied creatively to the key problem, it hit with far greater force.)

"Our plant has to be able to handle the most extreme cold weather for long periods of time," the manager replied.

"How often, on the average, do you need maximum pressures in a given system?" Halliday persisted.

This question completed the exploratory part of the interview. The answer disclosed that the boilers were too big for about 80% of the season and might be costing more than two smaller boilers. "That was my first inkling of a real need for an efficient unit like ours," Halliday says.

With the prospect's attention riveted on his problem, Halliday now led him to a serious consideration of his own services. "From what you tell me," he said, "I'm sure we can work out a system that will cover your needs—with clean flues, no smoke and no waste of fuel. At the same time, it will relieve you of any worries about zoning changes.

"It will take a week or two to work out the plans with our engineers. Could I come back and discuss it with you then?"

He could, he did, and he made a big sale.

ONE-INTERVIEW SYSTEMS

Halliday worked a two-interview system: exploratory call first, selling interview later. What about one-interview salesmen?

They can adapt as in the use of observation. Carry on a two-interview sale *in effect,* by splitting the interview into two parts, the exploratory first, selling later. They will gain the same creative impact.

He Does It By Phone

And they can do it in telephone selling just as easily as face-to-face. Broker George Bernard, for one, uses exploratory inquiry to sell prospect-oriented investment plans. Customarily, he spends the first few minutes gathering facts, digging out problems. And the prospects love it.

Recently, he phoned Silvio Mangari, 35-year old accountant and father of four. Adroit inquiry spotlighted three key facts and problems.

1. Mangari's older children are in private high schools where tuition charges are already beginning to pinch.
2. His educational outlays will soar in a few years, when his sons reach university level. His salary may or may not cover those higher costs.
3. He has a five-figure bank account never yet put into investments. In addition, he can still put aside something from his pay.

This cleared the deck for selling. "From what you tell me," said broker Bernard, "you need a plan with two main objectives. First you want to put together enough of an estate to take care of those costs you see coming. Then you want to disburse the estate toward costs, but only gradually and as needed. Does that sound right to you?"

"It does make sense," said the prospect.

"Good. Because you're conservative, you would not be happy in a speculative play. So let's put your bank savings into a sound, slow-growing mutual fund. Then we'll sign you up for a monthly accumulative plan out of current salary. Tell me how much you'd like to put aside every month and we'll work it out."

And the sale was made. More significant was Mangari's parting comment. "You know, Mr. Bernard, I wasn't sure I should get into the market. But the careful way you checked out my needs and financial situation convinced me that your plan was really meant to help me."

And there's a point the hit-and-run salesman may overlook. Sure, he covers a lot of ground and talks himself into a lot of orders. But he'll never know how many lost sales could have been retrieved—just for the price of taking the prospect's needs to heart.

What About Inheritance Taxes?

A number of insurance agents were rebuffed, for example by a prospect who was well protected by a comprehensive insurance plan. One agent, however, prepared a creative query, one that pinpointed a problem the prospect had not reckoned with.

"Have you considered the dent Federal Estate Taxes will make in your estate, given today's tax rate?"

When the prospect admitted he hadn't, the agent put a second and simpler question. "Where will the tax money come from?"

Then he sold an additional $20,000 policy for tax-paying purposes.

One-interview systems or two, exploratory inquiry means extra sales— sales that would otherwise be lost.

Digging Out Hidden Problems

Nor is this the only case, by far, where personal or business problems lurk unsuspected beneath the surface. Just bringing them into the open often serves a constructive purpose—since awareness is the first step toward solution.

Sometimes you know the problem exists because of a preliminary investigation or on-the-spot observation. Tell him directly, however, and he may resent it—since it makes him look as if he doesn't know his own business.

Instead, you let the problem emerge as a product of *his* thinking. How? By posing questions which put him squarely on target.

This serves you additional advantage when a competitor is in the picture. For you avoid the onus of "competition-knocking" which often repels the prospect entirely.

Of Problems and Price Competition

Here is a case where the prospect was shopping around for the best water treatment contract. When the salesman for Acme called, the prospect remarked, "There's no point discussing this unless you can beat Empire's quote."

This salesman knew that Empire underpriced him. And he also knew that their price was based on a serious fault. But he was too canny a salesman to attack his competitor directly.

So ignoring the prospect's remark, he asked: "Are you considering dry or liquid scale remover?"

"Liquid is what they quoted me on."

"I see. Well, it's certainly true that liquid scale remover is faster and cheaper. But tell me, do they guarantee you against corroded metal parts?" (Good selling in every respect. He freely admits the merits of the competing service *before* he slips in the question that alerts the prospect to an unsuspected problem: corrosion.)

"Guarantee?" the prospect repeated. "Nothing was said about a guarantee against corrosion. Do you offer one?"

"No. In fact, we don't use liquid removers at all because they're a bit tricky to handle. They produce heavy fumes which can be dangerous if there's no air circulating. And those fumes corrode metal parts.

"That's why we use powdered removers. They're safer to handle, and they contain more effective inhibitors for the best protection of metals."

"When I finished," says this salesman, "the prospect was no longer thinking about price."

Creative selling may not *always* beat price, but it sure gives you a good run for your money.

Be a Good Listener

Asking about problems becomes an empty exercise unless you cultivate the art of *listening*. Charles B. Roth, in his book, *Professional Salesmanship*, tells an illuminating story about Saunders Norvell, an outstanding sales executive.

Early in his selling career, a bad sore throat forced Norvell to do a lot more listening than talking for a full week. Much to his surprise, he recorded more sales than in any previous week-long stretch.

Experimenting further, Norvell talked more on some days, less on others. Always, he scored higher on "listening days" than on "talking days."

Not that this would surprise the creative seller. He knows that prospects are more interested in *their* problems than in *his* services.

One million-dollar-round-table man opens every sale by asking probing questions about the prospect's family. Then he sits there quietly, attentive to every detail, interjecting brief clarifying queries where needed.

The prospect *feels* the salesman's concern in an almost physical manner. And he responds warmly to the program eventually suggested to him.

That the salesman earns a commission on the sale doesn't really matter. What counts is the way he unfolds a plan that addresses itself directly to the worries the prospect himself has expressed.

Because the salesman *listens,* his prospects buy.

Listen Actively

Keeping quiet is not the point. You listen to find out what's bothering the prospect—*then do something about it.*

WHEN IS ENOUGH?

Mapping out a creative approach rests first upon adequate investigation of customer or prospect problems. But what is adequate for one case may be inadequate for another. You can provide yourself with a rough and ready guide, however, by asking yourself a few question.

Are you prepared to make a constructive call? Do you know the *specific* needs of the prospects and customers you're going to sell? Can you give them a clear picture of how you can serve those needs to their satisfaction?

If you must say "no" to those questions, more exploratory work is indicated. If your answers come up "yes", you're ready to prepare a constructive call.

2. HOW TO PREPARE A CONSTRUCTIVE CALL

In approaching your prospect for the selling interview, you must see yourself primarily as a *problem solver, and get your customer to see you the same way.* That's the last, most vital step of the creative sell.

Problem solving takes many forms. You may show a prospect an unsuspected application of your service, suggest an alternate service, help *him* land an important sale. The possibilities are endless.

But the technique is always the same. You don't *sell* your plan as a *plan,* you offer it as a *solution* or a *step* toward solution of his problem.

He Didn't Sell a House

A real estate man called upon a young couple of modest means who were on the verge of buying a nice home from a rival agent. The property he was handling was more expensive and he hadn't a hope if he sold it as a house per se.

... He Sold a Solution

But he knew the couple had a problem—whether or not they were aware of it. For their little girl was only a year away from starting school—and to get there from the house her parents were considering she'd have to go through a dangerous crossing.

Several children had been hurt there; one had been badly crippled just a few weeks before the real estate man called. Bringing this problem to his prospects' attention, the real estate man sold a solution: a house (his) on the right side of the dangerous street.

Coping with the One-Interview System

The two-interview salesman generally has plenty of time to prepare a constructive call in the time period between his exploratory and selling interviews. But no matter how deftly the one-interview man splits his call into exploratory and selling halves—he's still left with the task of producing solutions right on his feet.

No doubt about it: as a one-interview man you must labor under a handicap. However, there's still plenty you can do.

1. *Prepare generalized solutions to recurring situations.*

In many intangibles fields, for example, sales are closed on the basis of securing favorable financing. Develop your sources for securing loans of all types and you can produce solutions out of the proverbial hat.

One insurance adjuster has built a lot of business on the strength of a solution to a recurring agent problem: training a new claims girl.

"I have repeatedly encountered this situation," he says. "So with the help of my office I organized evening training sessions for claims girls in local agencies. Starting with a review of standard fire contracts and forms, these sessions gradually cover every kind of risk the company insures. And we always warn the trainees *not* to commit the company to liability.

"Whenever I run into this problem, I immediately suggest these sessions as a solution to training difficulties. This has been a key factor in securing business."

2. *Build your knowledge of applications.*

Different annuity options can have a considerable effect on the retirement values of various insurance policies. An investment plan can be geared to the individual problems faced by prospects in different tax brackets. An insurance program can be coordinated with social security benefits or ignore them.

The more you know applications, the more you can come up with solutions in the minutes at your disposal as a one-interview salesman.

3. *Focus on ideas.*

When you *don't* have solutions to specific problems, a constructive call can be built around *ideas* which can help the prospect in other ways. But more on this in a moment.

THE AIM'S THE THING

Once you aim for it, you'll find yourself automatically looking for—and finding—ways of being helpful. The pull of your goal keeps you on the ball.

It Was a Great Day's Work . . . But No Sales

Stan Kellogg tells how he saw the light. "The great majority of sales," he says, "are made only because a salesman happens in on the same day or hour the prospect has started thinking about service. But you can't build a steady business on that kind of selling. I know, because I used to do it myself.

"One night, when I was relaxing in my hotel, I remember thinking that I had put in a big day's work: 9 calls and 140 miles. But I had to admit I hadn't sold one."

"Why not?"

"Turning it over in my mind, I reached a harsh conclusion: without being aware of it, I was making a series of time-wasting 'here-I-am-again' calls; calls with no other purpose except that I wanted some business.

"Right then and there I reviewed my next day's calls and worked out a way I might be helpful to each prospect and customer I was planning to see. I made three calls that day."

His Objective Alerted Him

Once they put their minds to it, most intangibles salesmen will agree, they can find some valuable idea to bring along for almost any prospect or customer. Nor does it have to tie in to what you are selling.

Paul Lamont, a broker who is completely sold on the idea of constructive objectives for each call, tells an instructive story. "I arranged an appointment with an engineer who told me he was planning to organize a company for the manufacture and installation of water purification equipment. To open the door to this account, I determined to find some way of being constructive.

"While waiting in the office of another customer, I spotted an engineering magazine devoted to municipal water supply. *I would never have picked it up had I not been alerted to every possibility by my calling objective.*

"Thumbing through the publication, I found an article describing a new, economical process for spreading a protective film over reservoir water. I had that article Xeroxed.

"When I finally called on my engineer prospect and presented the copy to him, he was delighted. And the sale practically closed itself."

Making Time to Prepare

Given the sophistication of the average commercial buyer, desirable blocks of business may often swing on very narrow advantages. By falling back upon the careful preparation of constructive calls, you can create such advantages for yourself.

As always, the amount of time you put into them is a matter of individual judgement. Not only the present order but the future potential must be considered.

Only you can decide. But remember. The *extra* care that goes into a problem-solving presentation can spell the difference between pushing yourself into the higher brackets and staying down with the crowd.

One Preparation . . . 50 Installations

Here, recurring situations raise their delightfully profitable heads once again. For a prepared problem solver for one prospect may pay off in multiples if it can be applied or adapted to the needs of other clients.

"I have made a survey of water rates in my territory," writes Alvin Canfield, who sells air conditioning systems, "and I can cite operating costs on all water-cooled equipment. I have also trained myself to become expert in the selection, piping and control of remote, multi-circuited condensers.

"All this began as part of my preparation for landing one of my biggest contracts. Because of this background knowledge, I have sold over 50 similar installations in this area with little or no extra work."

KNOW YOUR SOURCES

As a problem solver, you're as good as your sources of knowledge. A primary source—and an important one—is the printed word: the literature your company puts out, trade publications, the business sections of local newspapers, books, and the like.

But all too often, reading materials are short on applications data. And this makes for a dangerous information gap.

It's all a matter of record. More than 360 out of 450 buyers queried by *Purchasing,* felt that most salesmen know their products and services in a technical sense, *but don't know how to apply their knowledge to the customer's needs and problems.*

To gain an edge on the crowd, the successful salesman builds up his own applications file.

How? By being inquisitive, and by exchanging ideas with his fellow salesmen.

Building the "Inquiring Eye" Habit

One man I know does a wonderful job of building his own idea library. "However did you acquire so much useful knowledge?" I once asked.

"By being perpetually curious," he replied. "I never let a day go by without trying to learn something new, some way in which my services or I myself can help a prospect or customer.

"And I usually succeed—by turning an inquisitive eye on everything which looks potentially useful. Immediately I'll ask 'how' or 'why'—and the answers go into my idea book.

"I've got more than a dozen such notebooks. Every week or so, I review one or two of them."

"Has this work paid off?" I asked.

"It's the most profitable thing I've ever done. Many times these information books have helped me win out against the toughest competition.

"Even more important, it has helped me develop long-range relationships with customers. *They want to do business with me because they know I can help them when they need it.*"

Any alert intangibles salesman who supplements his reading with the "inquiring eye" habit on his daily rounds can have a dozen useful ideas on tap at any one time. Some of these are bound to be useful to one or another prospect on whom he calls.

Exchanging Ideas

The one best way to make creative selling a habit, is to exchange creative experiences with your fellow salesmen in your office contacts, at sales meetings, or in your hotel of an evening.

Should your contacts be minimal, you can still conduct your own private exchange by using the cases in this book as a foundation, for most of them have a constructive base.

As you read each one, you are in effect looking over the shoulder of an experienced salesman as he prepares for and carries out a constructive call. And most of them will have at least one general idea which can be adopted or adapted by you.

CAPSULE SUMMARY

The great majority of intangibles salesmen can increase their volume and earnings by preparing more creative approaches to their prospects and customers. This means two things, primarily: Get close to your prospect's problems—then help him solve them.

In almost every sale, you'll find one factor which may seem irrelevant to the salesman, but is the key to the order from the buyer's viewpoint. When you conduct a pre-call investigation, when you explore before you sell, by on-the-spot observation and well planned inquiry—you will, in most cases, put your finger squarely on that key factor.

You'll now be selling from a favorable position.

For the selling interview, switch your role from problem finder to problem solver. Not that you can always come up with constructive answers on your own, but you can certainly do it by talking things over with others in your firm or in the same field, by referring to appropriate literature, and by cultivating an "inquiring eye."

And you'll strengthen your position even more by aiming to walk into every selling interview with at least one idea your prospect will find useful. To develop an idea file, cultivate every source of knowledge available to you.

PART III

Developing Presentations
That Sell Intangibles.

5

How to Generate Interest
in an Intangibles Presentation

You may be making a cold call, keeping an appointment with a man you've pre-approached, seeing an old customer, or selling by phone. Whatever your situation, the first 30 seconds of your interview will often determine whether you make your sale—or lose it.

For a prospect automatically raises his guard when a salesman appears on the scene. Sure, he'll listen: but with one ear—and an eye on the clock. To improve your chances, you've got to win his undivided attention with a "door-opener," an opening shot that gets you in and gets you heard.

Simply Does It

Not that you need set off a string of firecrackers to announce your presence. Just address yourself directly to the prospect's needs. It's truly as simple as that.

Consider an interesting example reported by Carl Gompert, who represents a freight forwarding outfit. "Recently," he writes, "I was up against a man who was a tough nut to crack. I just couldn't get in to see him.

"I sweated for days trying to dream up some stunt that would open his doors to me. I even tried a few—but he was always 'too busy.'

"Finally, I sent a note into his office with this straight-forward appeal to self interest: 'Mr. Gorman, would you be interested in an idea that can save you upwards of $500 a month on unloading and handling costs? I'm here to show you how.'

"That did it; I got in with my story."

And that *will* do it more often than not—provided you can deliver on what you promise.

WORK OUT YOUR "DOOR-OPENER"—AND MEMORIZE IT

The most telling—and selling—presentations rarely, if ever, rest upon on-the-spot inspiration. Mostly they're planned in advance. For as famed statesman Lloyd George once wrote, "The surest road to inspiration is preparation."

That holds just as true for selling as it does for statesmanship. Here's how one of the top producers for an investment consulting service explains it:

"Your first job is to establish an air of confidence the moment you walk in the door. Such confidence will be based on knowledge of your product, awareness of your prospect's needs—plus the fact that you have a sound plan of attack. When you know *what* you are going to do and *how* you will do it, you can't help but display confidence."

True. And that air of assurance often rubs off on your prospect—predisposing him to listen.

Tell Him Who and Tell Him Why

The fastest way to lose your prospect is to evade the issue of who you are, whom you represent, and why you're there. So tell him, tell him fast, and tell him constructively.

1. *You tell him fast by giving your name and your company in your very first sentence.*

"Mr. Richards, my name is Maxwell Geismar. I represent F. W. Dodge and Company." This displays a simple dignity and respect for your calling which normally commands an equally respectful response.

2. *You tell him constructively by planting the thought of gain in his mind.*

"Mr. Hopkins, my name is George Lansing. I represent the Bakewell Company of Chicago. I'm here to show you how our leased shoe departments can bring in larger net gains at minimum risk to you. Would you like to see how our plan can fit into your operations?"

There's nothing mysterious about the favorable response to Lansing's thoughtfully conceived approach. For his direct appeal to "larger net gains" cuts right to the heart of the door-opening technique: get the prospect to listen.

But if your opening strategy is best planned beforehand, it need not be canned. For door-openers come in an infinite variety of shapes and sizes. This will become clear as we discuss in turn the four basic interest-arousing techniques:

    A. Open on a promise.

    B. Ask a question.

    C. Offer useful information.

    D. Use a third-party referral.

A. OPEN ON A PROMISE

As we have seen, your opening shot must do one major job: capture the prospect's undivided attention. And what surer way than by touching on the one matter that truly fascinates any buyer: "What's in it for me?"

Take this instructive before-and-after story.

BEFORE: *He Was Too Busy To Listen*

One morning a bank officer was calling on a local manufacturer to present a Payroll Savings Plan. "I'm here to show you exactly how it works," he said in winding up his opening remarks.

The prospect had been listening politely, his mind obviously on his own work. "Let's discuss it some time when I'm not so busy," he said vaguely.

Just as the banker was leaving, an office systems salesman walked in. Before the door closed, the banker heard him say: "Mr. Anderson, would you like to hear how you can save a minimum of $150 a month?"

"I sure would," said the manufacturer. "Have a seat."

AFTER: *He Even Had Time for Coffee*

Let the contact officer tell the rest of the story himself. "When I heard Mr. Anderson tell that man to sit down, I had to ask myself: 'Why was he too busy to listen to me?'

"Having heard the salesman's opening line, the answer stared me in the face. I hadn't considered my prospect's needs. Why should he stop what he was doing because *we* want to sell a plan?

"Being a stubborn cuss, I decided to try again. While I was waiting I worked out a new opening.

"When the other man left, I poked my head through the door and said: 'Mr. Anderson, on my way out I thought of a question I'd like to ask you.'

" 'Go right ahead,' he replied.

" 'How much time must be put into making up your payroll every week?'

" 'Oh, I'd say about nine to ten hours.'

" 'Would you be interested in a plan that would save you more than half that time—adding up to over four weeks of labor saved every year?'

" 'In this business,' the prospect replied, 'a savings of four weeks' time is worth considering. But I don't see how you can do it.'

" 'That's exactly what I want to show you. Could you take a few minutes for a cup of coffee while I tell you how our plan can save you those extra weeks—and also cut down on some of the headaches that crop up in payroll routine?' "

This time round, Mr. Anderson could and did spare the time.
Why?
For one reason only. By opening on a promise, the banker convinced him he stood to gain something by listening.

"We Have a Plan . . . "

In most cases you won't get a second chance. That's why it makes sense to work out your opening shot before you call. Alex Somers will testify to that.

Alex sells mortgages in central Texas. Because many of his potential buyers are private investors who have never bought discounted mortgages, they fall more properly under the heading of suspects than of prospects. This makes the door-opening problem as difficult for Alex as it is important.

Yet here too, Alex finds that a candid appeal to self-interest gets him in more often than not. "Mr. Greenfield, we have a plan which many men in your situation are using to fill out the security side of their investment portfolios. May I have a few moments of your time to tell you what this plan can do for you?"

Sure, you've heard it before. Insurance men and mutual funds salesmen in particular find it a mainstay. For who wants to take a chance of missing out on something good?

But simple as it is, Alex points out that he never made the most of this opening promise until he committed it to memory. "It sounds easy enough. Yet somehow I always got off on a tangent when I was face-to-face with my prospect. Finally, I had to admit to myself that too many of my sales were sliding out from under because of my weak, off-the-cuff openings. That's when I sat down and worked this one out."

Keep It Affirmative

Harvey Bates used to open on this note when selling the services of a firm of consulting engineers: "Mr. Drake, I'd like to tell you why we feel we can do a good job for you."

That "we feel . . . " hardly carries much conviction. A flat assertion makes a sharper impact. Nor does it leave a hard-sell after-taste—provided you immediately go on to prove your claim. "We *can* do a good job *because* . . . ."

B. ASK A QUESTION

As an outstanding securities salesman puts it: "There's one best way to boost your sales: make every call a planned call. Some of the considerations that will prompt a given prospect or customer to respond well to your offerings can be determined in advance. You can dig out the rest during your call *if* you're prepared with a sufficient stock of questions.

"Before I myself fully absorbed this selling philosophy, I would limit myself to one or two opening queries. All too often, I failed to get to the heart of a prospect's problems. Nor could I guide his thinking along lines which would benefit both him and me.

"Now I write down as many as a dozen leading questions in preparing for a call. I may not use them all. I may even change the 'script' entirely if something new comes up.

"But one thing I'm sure of. However the interview may go, I'll still be on top of the situation."

A Soft-Sell Pattern

Analyze the presentations of this top producer and a distinct softsell pattern emerges: a pattern shaped by his preplanned line of inquiry. One question deftly plants a seed of desire, another draws out a key fact about the prospect's needs, a third uncovers some hidden resistance, a fourth deftly underscores a major buy point, while a fifth leads the prospect gently to the dotted line.

5 WAYS TO MORE SALES

The preplanned query helps you land more sales in five important ways. These take a certain amount of finesse. The best way to acquire the skill is to analyze the good and not-so-good examples of opening technique which will illustrate each point in turn.

1. Stay "You-Minded"

When calling on an agent to solicit more casualty business, insurance adjuster Ted Wohl opened fire like this: "Vic, our records show we've been getting a good share of your assignments, but practically all of it has been in casualty and auto claims. Of course, we appreciate the business, *but we want to develop more growth in fire and allied lines.* I'd like to discuss that with you today."

"Make it some other time, will you? I'm too busy now."

The italicized phrase is a good—or rather, a horrible—example of the self-centered approach a salesman may often slip into unawares. Why should a prospect jump for joy because "we want to develop . . . ?"

That shows, in the first place, where asking a question fits in. For you would hardly *ask* a prospect: "Would you like to discuss why we want to develop . . . ?" Phrased as a question, the egg-laying qualities of this approach stick out like a sore thumb.

See what happens, instead, when a salesman tackles the identical issue in query form. Both presentations, by the way were taped at the point of sale by researchers from the New York University School of Marketing.

"Vic, while I was waiting in your office, I happened to pick up one of your advertising folders. I take it that fast and efficient loss service is the heart and soul of your business."

"Are you kidding? I couldn't stay ahead of the game without it."

"Then let me ask you this: Did you ever stop to think that with our country-wide organization we can do a better job for your insureds, boost your reputation, and give you the same competitive edge on fire and allied claims that we now give you on casualty and auto losses?"

"How can you boost my reputation?"

Vic's question demonstrates that Wohl's query-based opening had achieved its goal. For now the agent was *listening*. And the more they listen, the more they'll buy.

Note how in this case, the salesman could zero in on the agent's main interests with a statement—"I take it that"—which is in itself an implied question. Then he underlines his "you-minded" tack by casting his promise in query form. This, as we have just seen, has the added virtue of softening what might otherwise seem to be somewhat brash claims.

Nor was all this accidental. For the same salesman was involved in both cases. After analyzing the tape of his original presentation, Ted Wohl was well motivated to sit down, prepare, and memorize this far more effective door-opener.

2. Dig Out the Key Buy Points

Often you start with some clue to the prospect's needs. Thus, a carefully designed question or two will help you underline the main selling point. Once it is firmly implanted in the prospect's mind, you can shape the rest of your presentation accordingly.

Consider what happened in the above case. When the agent asked, "How can you boost my reputation?" Ted knew he had hit upon the key point. So he immediately expanded upon that theme.

"You know we have the training and experience to make first-call settlements without waiting for an estimate from a repairman. That gives your insureds the fastest possible inspection and closing. What better advertising can you get?"

"None, I guess."

Ted could make the point himself by saying flatly, "You can get no better advertising." But by putting it as a question, he softens the effect—and lets the agent sell himself with his "None, I guess."

LISTEN BEFORE YOU LEAP

Naturally enough, a good salesman is always eager to tell his story. So all too often he dives right in without probing the prospect's mind first. Accordingly, he may fail to tailor his presentation to the prospect's real interests.

As one industrial buyer wryly remarks. "Salesmen often miss the most important comments I make. They're so engrossed in what *they* have to say, they hardly hear me at all."

While this may exaggerate the case, it does point up a sound moral. For sometimes what you suspect may be the chief selling point is not at all what most interests the prospect. But his response to your queries will surely put you on the right track—*if* you listen.

That's where asking questions pays off doubly. It not only pre-disposes him to listen to you—it forces *you* to listen to *him!*

CHANGING IN MID-STREAM

"Mr. Rockwood," said management agent Paul Gessner, "I'm sure you've heard about the kind of job we've done for other landlords. But have you ever considered how our 5-point management system can take all the servicing headaches off your shoulders, while at the same time assuring your tenants of the fastest possible response to complaints and repair requests?"

(With his question, Gessner directs attention to the main issue —as he conceives it).

"I'm always interested in satisfying my tenants. But my maintenance crew has full authority to react to any complaints immediately, and that ends it. However, the way prices have been rising, I am concerned about keeping my costs down."

(The prospect's answer shows that fast service is *not* the selling point in this case. But the query does bring out the real issue: keeping costs down. And Gessner comes to grips with it at once —with more inquiry).

"Would it be correct to say that your major expenses trace back to structural repairs?"

"That's right."

"Then don't you think our 5-point system might add up to substantial savings if we can catch potential damage before major repairs are necessary?"

"Could be; why don't you tell me how it works?"

Once you dig out the key buy point by really listening—you're well on your way to the sale. But doesn't it take a lot of experience to create such queries then and there?

Not necessarily. For as this salesman points out, if you've prepared your main line of inquiry beforehand, you're mentally geared to move in any direction the prospect may take you.

3. Focus On His Problems

In Chapter 4, we saw why a constructive call—where you place the prospect's problems in the center of the stage—is perhaps the most powerful weapon in the salesman's armory. And we saw too that most salesmen have more sources of information on prospect problems than they may be aware of.

However, no matter how well you prepare, you're bound to have blind spots in your knowledge of a given prospect's needs. There's one best way to remove them: ask questions designed for the purpose. The more pains you take with queries obviously meant to help them, the more your prospects will tend to sell themselves on the desirability of dealing with you.

"I NEED A FEW MORE DETAILS"

Earlier, we referred to the opening promise made by Don Robinson, who sells leased shoe departments. Once he wins the prospect's ear, Don slams on the brakes.

"Before I can be sure that a leased department makes sense for you, Mr. Greenfield, I need some details about your operation. Do you mind if I ask you some questions?"

> (The implication that the service must have real value for the prospect before he will press for the sale, invariably insures a respectful hearing.)

Don now follows up with his preplanned line of inquiry. Have profits kept pace with volume? How do the operating expenses of the shoe salon compare to other departments? What is its share in the total advertising budget?

These and similar questions further the sale in two ways. First, they reinforce the feeling that Don will press for the sale only if the facts warrant it. Second, they help the prospect sell himself, for his every answer establishes in his own mind the potential value of the proposition.

And *don't* overlook the effect of that baited hook, "I need a few more details" to see if it "makes sense for you." For this primes the prospect to go along with queries into his personal or business problems.

HIS CUSTOMERS HELP HIM ASK

By cleverly combining skillful inquiry with a dramatic pause, Chet Brooks lets his prospects fan their own interest with the questions they toss at him. When he finally takes over and focuses on their specific problems, they're ready to give out with the facts he needs. This creative approach—prepared well before his call—has made Chet his firm's top producer.

Here is a typical example of Chet at work.

"Mr. Grimes, I'm Chester Brooks. I represent the Cinelab Industrial Communications Association."

Pause.

"Oh. Does your company make films?"

"In a way, but that's not our real job."

"What do you do then?"

"We solve problems."

Pause.

"Do you mean you can solve some of our problems with your films?"

Here Chet makes a quick switch and takes over the questioning. "That depends on the kind of problems you have. Tell me, Mr. Grimes, is your main problem in labor relations, manufacturing or selling?"

> (With his "that depends . . . " answer, Chet implies, as Don
> Robinson did: "I won't talk business with you unless you have
> the kind of problems we can do something about.")

"Right now I'd say we have a selling problem more than anything else."

"Does it lie in getting your salesmen to know your product better or in educating your distributors to merchandise it more aggressively?"

"I think they could both stand to know a lot more."

And so it goes. By the time he finished his queries, Chet had Mr. Grimes telling him exactly the kind of communications film his firm needed to solve its selling problem. Then Chet proceeded to sell him a contract.

As Chet puts it: "This problem-solving approach arouses interest because it makes sense. No prospect is interested in our films, he's interested in solutions. But I can't offer any solutions until I get close to his problems."

Nor must you work up a sweat searching for "clever" questions. As all our cases indicate, it's the implied benefit or the expression of concern that counts—*not* the originality of phrasing. Chet's dramatic pause and Don Robinson's "I need a few more details" are merely subtleties of application that come with practice.

4. Uncover Hidden Resistance

You can't sell if your prospect is nursing some unstated objection. That's why some seasoned representatives will insert a query designed to smoke out one or another of these hidden barriers before they launch into their main story. Once they get past the opening roadblock, they believe, the prospect will be more strongly inclined to lend a sympathetic ear.

Normally, I would not seek out resistance until the prospect has absorbed some part of the benefits picture. For at that time, an objection can be more readily overcome. But where you're running up against a residue of complaints or resistance carried over from the past, your story is bound to go in one ear and out the other unless the barrier is effectively removed.

And that can't be done until you know exactly what you're facing.

"IS THERE ANY SPECIFIC REASON . . . ?"

How to handle resistance will be covered quite fully when we come to Chapter 7. Should you be faced with that kind of situation, it is sufficient at this point to note how Al Sloan does it. When calling on a former customer, for example, Al was sure the man was harboring some grudge against his company. So Al asked: "Is there any specific reason why you've stopped using our service?"

Sure enough, the man opened up—giving Al his chance to smother the objection in a strong solution of benefits.

5. Help Him Sell Himself

Plenty of people just don't like to be told, or sold. No matter how much they stand to gain, if you tell them flatly: "I think you ought to try . . ." you may well lose them.

Where a prospect resents being told, a broad question of opinion which invites *him to talk* may work when nothing else will.

Here is an amusing case in point. Many years ago, when William Wrigley, Jr. started his career as a soap salesman, he stumbled onto the value of this technique.

For in all innocence, he walked into a store whose proprietor hated the firm Wrigley represented, and asked for an order.

"You and your company can go jump in the river," the grocer snarled.

Young Wrigley started to close his kit, "I guess there's no point trying to sell you," he said mildly. "But I'm a new salesman and I wonder if you would give me some pointers. What do you think I might say to other prospects in order to make more sales?"

"My lad," the grocer began—and went into a 15-minute lecture on how to sell those very soaps he had turned down. You guessed it: he made such a good job of it—he sold himself!

LET THEM TALK

That's how young Wrigley learned a very important lesson. The man you can't sell may sell himself—if you give him a chance to talk.

Most people love the sound of their own voices. Ask their advice, as Wrigley did, and the dam will frequently burst.

THE OPINIONATED DOCTOR

Many intangibles salesmen who have never heard the Wrigley story apply the same technique: more subtly, perhaps, but none the less successfully. As in this case.

"I have been taking care of my business affairs long enough to look after my own estate," a physician said smugly to a salesman who had just explained he was there to discuss an estate-planning service.

"Of course," the salesman agreed, deftly sidestepping argument. "But, Dr. Groves," he went on, "a busy man can sometimes miss a trick or two. Do you think a point-by-point check of your estate might be a wise bit of insurance?"

"Point-by-point check? What's that?"

(The salesman's first query succeeds in arousing interest).

"One of our new features: we analyze the present composition of your estate—paying special attention to tax vulnerability; examine your portfolio; and make detailed recommendations for improving the condition of your estate. I wonder what your opinion is about such an independent check?"

(Here the salesman uses a more sophisticated version of the Wrigley method. By asking the doctor's opinion, he gives him a chance to talk himself into the sale—and the doctor did a good job of it, too.)

"Dr. Groves was somewhat opinionated," the salesman reminisces. "Had I not aroused his interest with my prepared line of inquiry, I am sure he would not have listened to another word."

Opinionated or not, we all like to express our points of view. The more you pepper a man with queries designed to let him talk, the greater the chances that you'll help him sell himself.

HE INQUIRED HIS WAY TO THE MILLION DOLLAR CLUB

Bob Olsen sells life insurance. In his early days as a salesman he got down to the point where he had to borrow to eat. His friends advised him to give up; he was no salesman, they told him.

But Bob discovered what a few simple questions can do. For years, now, he's been a member of the exclusive Million Dollar Round Table. Here's one example of how he literally inquires his way to the sale.

"Mr. Graham, my name is Bob Olsen. I represent the John Hancock Company. I'm here to talk to you about life insurance."

"I'm sorry; I can't possibly afford to buy any more insurance."

(It was this initial resistance that had always stymied Bob until he learned to bypass it with a series of soft-sell questions).

"But supposing you did buy some more—would you want it for savings or for protection?"

(Probing for the prospect's key buy point).

"That's easy. We have a new baby now, so I'd want it for protection, to make sure he gets through college whatever happens."

Now Bob centers on the established buy point. "College is a real necessity these days, and you can't start preparing for it too early. But when you consider the inflationary pressures in our economy, doesn't it make sense to add a precautionary edge against runaway prices?"

"I guess you're right but I don't see how I can do it."

"Let's say you saw your way clear, how much additional protection would you take?"

"Ten thousand dollars would be tops considering all my obligations."

"If anything happened to you, Mr. Graham, do you think your wife and child could get along without this extra $10,000?"

There was a long pause while the prospect thought that one over. "I guess they would need it," he said slowly, "if my kid is to have any real chance of getting into college."

"Since you see it that way, would you like to discuss a plan that will enable you to take on this extra protection now?"

"Let me hear what you have in mind."

Once again, Bob's well-planned line of inquiry had blazed a trail from attention-getting opener to successful close. Since this was uncommonly good selling, let us briefly analyze Bob's technique.

1. All his questions were "you-minded": "would you want it for savings or protection?" and so on.

2. He let the selling idea, the need for extra protection, become the *prospect's* idea. This merits closer examination.

   Notice how he asked first: *"Doesn't* it make sense . . . ?"

   With that question he was fishing for agreement—which every salesman wants at the outset.

   But when he switched to *"Do you think* your wife and child could get along . . . ?" he appealed completely to the other man's opinion. *Thus the answer becomes the prospect's own idea.* And because it's his idea, he'll more likely stick with it.

   Finally, Bob neatly drove home the "this-is-your-idea" strategy with his: "Since you see it that way . . . ."

Anyway you look at it, this was a masterly job of selling. And that's how Bob Olsen made the Million Dollar Club—with prepared questions that arouse interest, dig out the key buy points—then lead his prospects to the close.

C. OFFER USEFUL INFORMATION

Why does one salesman succeed where another one fails?

Let a buyer answer that one. Responding to a survey conducted by *Purchasing* magazine, the Director of Purchasing of I.B.M. put it this way: "One word is the key to why one salesman makes the sale where another one doesn't: 'preparation.' The salesman who makes the sale is the one who is prepared to give the buyer all the information he needs to buy intelligently."

The Extra Step

Most tangibles salesmen do arm themselves with relevant information before making their calls. But I'm talking about the *extra* step: the step that gives you a competitive edge.

This may take the form of supplying information directly tied to what you're selling: a new stock offering, details on a personal retirement plan —or it may not. Either way, if it's information which helps the prospect solve a personal or business problem, it's a sure fire door-opener.

For example, a salesman who sells a tax information service learned that an important prospect had a tight cash situation. That salesman knew some of the possible answers: better and quicker collections and better inventory control.

Before he called, however, he took an extra step. In consultation with his home office and his bank, he prepared a 10-point check list of ways to stretch the prospect's cash flow. This constructive approach eventually solved the prospect's problem—and gained an account for the helpful salesman.

Reverse Inquiry

In Chapter 4 we discussed how you can go about collecting all the information you may need about and for a given prospect or customer. But once you know the facts, you may often want a soft-sell way of getting them across to the prospect's mind. Here again, asking a question can serve the purpose.

A salesman who was trying to sell a business insurance plan to a partnership heard from a reliable source that the principals were somewhat worried about the future of the business. However, he did not want to reveal his knowledge, nor did he want to be too blunt in suggesting they do something to secure the future.

His solution? He asked: "Have you ever considered how this business could be carried on if either partner were incapacitated?"

You might call this "reverse inquiry." *You* know the facts, but you inquire so that *the prospect* can learn them painlessly or "inform" you under his own head of steam. At the same time, the question softly injects a promise into the picture.

Not that reverse inquiry need be limited to potentially embarrassing situations. It can be used wherever a soft-sell approach seems indicated or is preferred.

Even when your query doesn't really say very much, it can still arouse the prospect's interest if it seems to be imparting information. For example, Cy Havermeyer, a salesman in the mutual funds field, reports that the following information-dropping query serves as a good door-opener even though it says very little. "Mr. Mack, did you know that only a very small percentage of the people who own stocks and bonds do their own studying of the market?"

While this works for him, you will probably do best by devising questions which do offer useful information—something that will make the prospect think—and if his thoughts lead him to contemplation of your services, so much the better.

D. USE A THIRD-PARTY REFERRAL

Probably the fastest way to warm up a cold call is to slip a third-party referral into your opening remarks. Take the case of Basil Read, who sells investment services to banks. Assigned to introduce his firm's services in an area where very few bankers had been exposed to them, Read had a real door-opening problem on his hands.

Here is how he broke through the opening barrier when approaching the bank presidents who were his prospects. After the usual amenities, Read would say: "Our various investment advisory services are used by several thousand banks across the country.

"Some banks in this area are on our client list because they heard about us from bankers back East or on the coast. For example, I'm sure you know Mr. Greeley down in Phoenix. Well, his bank has been using our services to good advantage for the past year."

Note that Read employs two interest-arousing devices.

    1. He makes a *general* third-party reference, the many banks "across the country" which use his services.

    2. He strengthens the impact with a *specific* third-party referral, a bank in the prospect's own area which is currently using these services "to good advantage."

Make Sure It's For Real

Of course, if you bluff the referral, if your services are *not* as widely used as you claim—then you may be building up to a very hard fall. But where it's real, this kind of two-pronged referral is the key to opening doors when you must make a cold call.

It comes as no surprise to find that in quite a number of his calls Read got this kind of response from the banking executives he dealt with:

"Oh, yes, Mr. Read, I heard about your services at the recent Bankers' Convention and I've been meaning to write to your company. But you know how it is; we get so busy we forget to do these things. However, I'm glad to see you now. Won't you come in?"

Get a Direct Referral, When You Can

When you can get a satisfied customer to refer you directly to a given prospect—you're in. For this kind of approach almost always achieves your opening objective: get an interview.

"Mr. Bridges, I'm Stanley Addison of Universal Freight Forwarding Services. Jim Boyle over at Baumer Manufacturing Company suggested that I call on you and tell you what we have been able to do for *his* company and how we can do the same kind of job for you."

Regardless of what you sell, it's a rare prospect who will turn down your bid for an interview when you come along with a *personal* third-party reference. How can you get referrals of this type?

The answer is clear: ask a satisfied customer. It won't always work; but just as a satisfied customer is your best lead to new prospects, he is equally your best source for direct referrals.

Convert Your Pre-approach

When you or your firm have sent mailings to a prospect, you can refer to that warm-up contact as though it were a third-party referral. A number of salesmen have found that this type of referral serves as a useful door-opener when they follow up such mailings with a personal call.

Consider a typical example. "Mr. Waldman, my name is Dick Cranston. I represent the Silas Deane organization of Denver. We have a plan for training salesmen which a good many companies in situations similar to yours are using to get their new men into the field quickly and productively.

"You recently received some mail on this subject from the president of our company and I am here to describe how our plan can be adapted to your needs. May I come in?"

There are two good reasons why this door-opener has secured a good percentage of interviews.

1. Cranston faithfully follows the third-party referral technique. First he uses a general referral: "which a good many companies (like) yours are using." Then he follows up with his specific referral: the letter "from the president of our company."

2. He reinforces these referrals with two strong opening promises. This training service "gets new men into the field quickly and productively." And when he adds, "I am here to describe how our plan can be adapted to your needs," he makes an implied promise to tailor the program to the prospect's specific situation.

On the Telephone, Too

Grant Pendill sells securities mostly by phone. Yet he uses precisely the same technique when he follows up his mailing with a telephone call.

"Mr. Bascomb, my name is Grant Pendill of Merrill, Lynch, Pierce, Fenner and Smith. You recently received a letter from me describing a new plan which many investors are using to build a balanced portfolio for both immediate gains and long range security. I'm calling now to see how we might best fit that plan to your circumstances."

Once again we see the same four ingredients that work so well in opening doors for selling any type of intangible.

1. The general referral: many investors.

2. The specific referral: the letter from me.
3. The general promise: immediate gains and long range security.
4. The "just for you" promise: we fit the plan to your circumstances.

IN A NUTSHELL

When you get in and get heard, you've achieved your opening objective and taken your first big stride toward landing your order. And you'll do the job best when you work out and memorize a door-opening strategy before you call.

Don't reach for something fancy. *Do* slant your opening toward your prospect's needs and interests. And build it around the four basic interest-arousing pathways:

Open on a promise.

Ask a question.

Offer useful information.

Use a third-party referral.

6

How to Move the Sale Along
with a Problem-Solving Approach

When you open on a promise, when you ask a question geared to dig out your prospect's buy points, when you focus on his problems—you've automatically been getting "you-minded."

That's the beauty of it. To make the most of your opening strategy, you've had to think and talk about the *buyer's* wants and needs. All of which takes you well on your way toward really talking benefits.

And it's talking benefits which moves the sale along toward the close.

THE BENEFIT TWINS

What's the key to more and better sales? Every salesman knows the answer.

"Sell the benefits!" they will tell you.

Yet it costs us money every day in sales needlessly lost because we don't practice what we know.

Why do experienced salesmen sometimes miss the boat?

Precisely because they're so wrapped up in their products and services —as all good salesmen must be. For unless you think about it carefully, it's all too easy to confuse technical *description* with customer *benefits*.

"Mister, Will It Keep Me Warm?"

Consider the classic story of the salesman out to sell a heating plant to an elderly lady. He waxed enthusiastic about construction features, talked about B.T.U.'s, thermostats, and automatic damper controls.

Then, when he paused for breath, the little old lady came up with this wonderfully human question: "Tell me, mister, will it keep me warm?"

Sell the Benefit—Not the Product

To put it bluntly, your prospect doesn't give a hoot about your goods or services—but he'd sure like to know what they can *do* for him.

Generally speaking, your service can *save*: time, money, labor, and the like.

Or it can *give*: more production, profits, efficiency, safety, security, et al.

Organize your thinking and talking around those benefit twins—*saving* and *giving*—and you're bound to hit squarely on the target far more often.

When you say, for example: "Under our Business Security Plan, the life values of an executive of 40 can be insured over a 20-year period at an average net cost of only $25 a year," you're being a John Hancock technician.

But suppose you translate that into: "Our Business Security Plan will strengthen your firm's cash assets and credit position."

Now you're being a John Hancock salesman.

A Matter of Viewpoint

At a sales meeting where the little old lady story had just been told, one man said: "I'm sure all experienced salesmen describe the virtues of their products or services."

"Yes," shot back another, "but from whose viewpoint? I used to fall into the description trap myself even after years of selling. Take the time, study and cost analysis plan I've been pushing these past couple of years.

"Just by describing the plan with all the enthusiasm I felt for it, telling the prospect about the 5-man team we'd farm out to him and the flow charts they'd develop as they followed our system, I would put across the point that this might be a good deal. Sure, these were virtues—but from our viewpoint, reflecting the pride we felt in a system we had originated.

"But now I make *more* sales—and more simply—by selling the benefit from the prospect's point of view. That is, I pound away with those savings and giving twins we've just discussed.

"I tell him how our plan will *save* him money by eliminating or cutting down on certain concealed costs which every multiple product firm we've studied has overlooked. And I emphasize the extra profit he'll *gain* because our plan will help him concentrate on those items which carry the biggest profit ticket."

Remember that tag line: "Mister, will it keep me warm?"—and you'll never fail to tell your prospect how your services can help him save or gain. And that's all we mean when we say: "Sell the benefit—not the product."

FOUR WAYS TO MAKE THE MOST OF BENEFITS

What you want to sell may vary; whom you want to sell may vary; but always the benefits techniques remain the same. You must apply them carefully, however, to fit each varying situation.

That does require thought and planning. How you do it will gradually emerge as you consider the four ways benefits will help you move the sale along.

A. Prepare a "benefits brief."
B. Sell the benefit the prospect wants.
C. Sell the differences.
D. Wrap up each major buy point as you move along.

A. PREPARE A "BENEFITS BRIEF"

Analyze any well designed selling story. You'll find it breaks down into several distinct buy points. Each moves the prospect closer to the sale, once implanted in his mind. Yet, as various point-of-sale studies reveal, most salesmen persistently overlook some of the potent selling points so carefully built into the presentation.

Curiously enough, different salesmen in the same firm will leave out different ones; though a point passed up by one man proves quite effective in the hands of another. Asked why they invariably ignore buy points that could help them close more sales, most come up with some variant of: "I guess I got into the habit of doing it that way."

Add up a sale lost here, another gone there and you've got a habit that costs you dearly. And that's precisely where a "benefits brief" comes into the picture. Prepared beforehand, it virtually eliminates such oversights.

HOW TO DO IT

To prepare your brief, you follow a simple, three-stage process.

1. List Every Major Buy Point

To do the job properly, you've got to be encyclopedic at this stage. Not that you'll relentlessly plod your way through your entire armory of selling points at every interview. Often you'll have some idea of the prospect's interests before you walk in the door and you'll mold your story accordingly.

Even when you have no line on the prospect, you'll generally pick up a clue as the interview progresses. And with your benefits brief at your fingertips, you'll never be caught flatfooted.

Today, you zero in on this benefit, forget that one. Tomorrow, you skip the first, give the second the full treatment. With the full range of your story to choose from, you never need fear that you'll lose the prospect for want of a convincing clincher.

2. Work Out a Logical Sequence

Many salesmen who fear that a carefully outlined presentation will repel the prospect with its patently canned rigidity, pitch in and and sell without knowing where they're heading from one sentence to the next. They often lose their prospect—and their sale.

True, a fresh spontaneity sparks enthusiasm in salesman and prospect alike. But a *planned* story need *not* be a *canned* one. With a benefits brief coupled to a well plotted sequence, you're always on top of the situation— leaving you free to tell your story in your own freshly-minted words.

Now, however, interruptions rarely throw you off. Despite phone calls and people popping in and out of the room, you can always pick up the thread of your story with no loss of time or equilibrium.

What's more, your story now flows with a cumulative impact that often makes buying the only logical conclusion.

When planning your sequence, give special attention to your opening and closing shots. Your opening benefit should be powerful enough to gain your prospect's undivided attention. Your closing one should set him up for the sale.

HE HELD OUT TO THE VERY END

Many salesmen like to start with the point of maximum interest. Yet in some cases, where your judgement so indicates, you may want to reserve your major benefit for the climactic moment when you're heading for the order.

Consider the battle for the elevator-installations contract for the 42-story Socony Vacuum building in New York. Two giant corporations slugged it out for the prize, matching blow for blow at every step in the long-drawn-out negotiations.

Specifications were virtually the same; so were the price bids. However, one firm had just developed an exclusive: an electronic device that keeps a closing door from even touching a protruding arm or leg. Since the installation was to be completely automatic, this had a strong sales appeal.

But the vice-president handling negotiations for the firm cannily played it close to his chest. If he turned up this hole card too early, he felt, his competitor might somehow minimize it.

Waiting until the bids had been opened and the Socony people were in conference with the contractors, he sent in word of his new device with a final closing string attached: "I think potential tenants will like this safety feature."

His firm walked off with the contract.

Granted, this was exceptional. But the principle still holds. Feed each buy point into your presentation at a carefully calculated time and place and you'll give yourself an important competitive advantage. And that's all any salesman can ask for.

3. Assemble Sufficient Back-Up Material to Support the Validity of Each Major Buy Point

Since selling the benefits is perhaps the most universally applied salesmanship principle, your prospects will be getting a steady diet of buy points from your competitors as well as from you. This creates a certain amount of skepticism which makes the most outstanding benefit just a claim, until your prospect accepts it as true.

That's why you must take your benefits brief one step further. You've got to convert each point from unsubstantiated claim to living reality. For the most part, you can do this best in one of two ways:

First by using figures, and second, by force of example.

USING FIGURES

Everybody understands simple figures—and many can be swayed by them. In some cases, the use of figures can validate a buy point faster and more clearly than any other method.

And you can strengthen your case with a bit of psychology, as well. That is, let your prospect put the figures on paper himself. Because they then become "his"—even though you supply or suggest most of them— his skepticism crumbles.

Some leading life insurance agents do this as a matter of course. The same idea can be adapted to many presentations.

One salesman uses this method to good effect when dealing with tough-minded industrial buyers. He sells spectrometers designed to determine the proper mix of metals for electric furnaces with the least loss of time.

This salesman walks in on his prospects armed with a simple form to list the various savings the spectrometer makes possible. Handing the form to the buyer, foundry superintendent or whomever, he suggests that the prospect estimate the savings.

"To begin with," says the salesman, "the spectrometer eliminates trips to and from the laboratory and minimizes down time." Whereupon the prospect estimates the savings this represents and lists it in the appropriate place on the form: under "down time savings."

So it goes from beginning to end. As the prospect estimates the dollar savings *he himself works out in accordance with the salesman's claims,* these claims become more and more real to him. The total savings figure is all the more impressive since he now sees it as his own—even though each item in it flowed directly from the salesman's benefit brief.

THE FORCE OF EXAMPLE

The automobile salesman can let his man get behind the wheel. The intangibles salesman can validate his claims—if less directly—with the playback of real-life stories of customer satisfaction.

HIS CARD FILE PAVES THE WAY

One insurance salesman, John Heller by name, converts his benefits brief from a string of unsubstantiated claims to a documented list of advantages, with the help of a thick stack of 3 x 5 file cards. Each card is headed by a major buy point, like this one: "Fast claims handling." To document the claim, he writes up one or two cases on the same card.

Most insurance men offer prompt claims handling as a key benefit. But having memorized his back-up stories, John milks the claim for all it's worth.

"Our company has a long standing policy," he'll say. "We handle all claims promptly and to the customer's satisfaction. Just a short time ago, for example . . ." and he brings the claim alive with a true story of an emergency situation handled on the heels of an urgent, middle-of-the-night phone call.

As John explained it to me: "Some of my stories have a negative slant. Many people respond well to this—buying or strengthening an insurance program in order to avoid the disasters visited upon the man who neglected his insurance needs.

"Other stories take a positive bent, showing how a planned insurance program helped a man caught in an otherwise sticky situation. For each interview I choose the kind of story I think will go best in the given situation."

HOW TO BUILD YOUR OWN BACK-UP FILE

"How many of these stories do you have on file?" I asked.

"In my five years in the business I have collected a little more than 60 stories. That amounts to an average of about five for each major selling point."

"Where do you get them from?"

"Some come from my own experience with my clients. Others come from swapping stories with other men in my office. And a good number come from reading trade publications. *Every time I run across a story I feel I can use to good effect, I clip it and add it to my 3 x 5 file.*"

PUTTING YOUR BACK-UP FILE TO WORK

"That certainly sounds like a fine idea," I said. "Now exactly how do you put that file to work for you?"

"Well, Mr. Smith, I begin with the calls I have scheduled for the day.

First I review what I know about the various prospects or customers I'm seeing that day, choosing the selling points I think will do the trick in each case. Then I put the appropriate cards in the order in which I want to make my points. Finally, I pick the one or two stories I feel will come closest to the situation of the man I'm going to see. I call these 'comparable situation' cards."

"Then you don't plan on using a story for each buy point you're going to stress?"

"Not usually; it would stretch the presentation out too long. But I *review* the stories on each card so that I can throw another one or two into the hopper should I be having a tough time convincing the prospect.

"At this point, I combine my cards with the notes I have made for my general approach, my opening and closing strategies, what resistance I can anticipate, and the like. Then I review the entire scheme the last few minutes before my appointment—in my car, in the lobby of the prospect's office building, or in front of his home. A last flip-through of the stories I've chosen for that interview, and I'm ready for the sale."

THE PAYOFF

Maybe it sounds like a lot of trouble. But it pays off big. Together with his meticulously prepared presentation strategy, Heller's file card benefits brief sees him through the most difficult selling situations.

Not long ago, while phoning for an appointment, a prospect told him he was sending for information about a nationally advertised low-premium policy. "Working against that price differential wasn't easy," John says, "but guided by my file, I built a presentation around one basic theme: the value of a balanced plan geared to future needs, as well as to the present. And only the constant, personalized attention of a local insurance man could develop that kind of plan with coverage adequate for any contingency.

"Then I punched the point home with the story of a man who insured his car, for himself and his son as drivers, at bargain rates. But when his son was involved in a serious accident while driving a neighbor's car, he found that his low-cost protection was also inadequate protection, for the policy did *not* cover his son while he was driving someone else's car."

In some states this story might not apply, but the principle still holds good. A negative story, showing the disaster that results from inadequate coverage is one of the best ways of overcoming a price-differential.

With such stories from his ever-expanding inventory of cases, young Heller made the Million Dollar Round Table in his second year as a salesman. His earnings have exceeded $20,000 for three years running, his third, fourth and fifth years in the business. "You can safely predict that John's income will soon top the $30,000 mark—and more," his manager confides.

Maybe it's worth the trouble.

B. SELL THE BENEFIT THE PROSPECT WANTS

Not all benefits are of equal value to every prospect. One man reacts to price, a second seeks security, while a third goes for the speculative gamble.

The moral? Simply this: the benefit which is of no interest to the man in front of you *is no benefit for that sale.*

Keep It Flexible

How can you tell which benefits will do the trick in a given case? That depends on how you operate.

If you work on the two interview system, your first exploratory call will dig out the prospect's real interests. In the one interview system, you've got to feel your way through—trusting to your prepared queries to put you on the right track.

However you do it, in pinpointing the right benefit for the right man, "flexibility" is the watchword. Drop *your* idea of the main benefits when *his* reactions indicate otherwise.

Even in midstream, a well-conceived query can help you switch horses in time.

He Was Selling Investment Counsel . . .

A salesman for a leading brokerage house offers a good case in point. "One morning," writes salesman Alvin Jenkins, "we received a post card request for our investment newsletter. Since this indicated the writer was a good prospect for our full investment services, I phoned the man at his office and told him I was pleased to put him on our mailing list.

" 'Are you in the market regularly?' I asked.

" 'Oh, yes.'

" 'Then I think you'd be interested in an account which assures you experienced and unbiased investment advice. Many of our customers tell us we have helped them improve their holdings no end. Would you like to discuss the matter in detail?' "

> (Jenkins opens up with what *he* assumes is a powerful buy point for this prospect)

. . . When The Prospect Wanted a Time Saver

" 'Frankly, I've been doing pretty well these past few years on my own,' he replied."

> (If you were too intent on what *you* considered important, you might miss your cue here: that investment *advice* was *not* this man's meat. But our man Jenkins wisely shifted gears).

"Quickly I dropped the 'investment counsel' gambit. To gain time for hitting on some other selling point, I asked if he wanted to receive the newsletter at his home, or if he preferred to look it over in the office.

" 'I never have a spare minute at the office,' he said. 'I'd appreciate getting the newsletter at home.'

"This sounded promising. So I asked. 'How come you're so busy?' "
    (Again we see how even in a one-interview sale, the first part of
    the interview can be handled as though it were an exploratory
    call).

"It seemed that the molded-rubber fabricating plant he owned had been steadily expanding. Keeping up with the orders took every minute of his time.

" 'Have you ever considered how an investment account might take some of your time-consuming chores off your back?' I asked him now.

" 'What do you mean?'

" 'For example, we can probably save you a big chunk of time just by handling your maturing investments. And we'd do a more thorough job of it, at that. Would you like to have lunch with me some time next week so that we can discuss it further?'

"Obviously, I had now hit on the right benefit for this man because he made an appointment for the following Monday. The upshot of it all was that he opened an account to the tune of $150,000."

Selling In Depth

When selling to industrials, a sale may rest upon a series of buying decisions from different departments, often at various levels of command. When negotiating such a sale, you must slant your story in a different way for each man you see.

Salesman Leonard Canfield would work out a highly specific benefit story for each firm he was prospecting—but that's as far as he'd go. Given the chance, he would happily recite the same story to everyone who'd lend him an ear.

"I wasn't pulling in enough sales," he says, "until I changed my approach. Now that I tailor my presentation to the specific man I'm dealing with, I take less time and *maintain more interest* at every phase of the negotiations.

"Just recently I was calling on a manufacturer of equipment for the crude oil industry who uses the services of a competitive water treatment firm. When talking to the Purchasing Director, I stressed the desirability of having another reliable company on tap as an emergency measure.

"In the engineering department I was out to prove that we could meet their exacting specifications while maintaining accurate quality control.

"And I took a different tack once more with top management. For at that level, I had to demonstrate that our services could and would have a favorable effect on costs and profits. By shifting focus as I went along, I gave myself a better chance for a favorable decision at each level."

That's it in a nutshell. Every man you must see—from purchasing agent to president—has his own areas of interest. Shape your story accordingly, and you'll stay on target every inch of the way.

C. SELL THE DIFFERENCES

"The trouble with my line," many a salesman will complain, "is that every firm in my field can boast exactly the same advantages—and at the same price. There's no benefit that I can offer that can't be matched by one of my competitors."

This does pose a problem. And all too often, the issue then turns on personality or contacts. The man who can make and keep friends more easily or who has an introduction to or from the right man, may well get the jump on his competitors.

But it is much more sound to build on the basis of differences *you can create for yourself.* The extra benefit that only you dream up will surely be unique to you and your organization. While a winning personality doesn't hurt, in business it's the extra benefit that makes more friends and influences more people.

How do you do it? You can create and sell important differences in three ways.

1. Remove your story from competitive comparisons.
2. Ring in the obvious.
3. Remember: you're part of the package.

1. REMOVE YOUR STORY FROM COMPETITIVE COMPARISONS

How do you remove yourself from competitive comparisons when battling against equal service and price? One good way is to start selling a different package—and I *don't* mean that you switch fields.

He Created His Own "Monopoly"

An example will make clear what I *do* mean. Insurance man Charles Kerr had long resigned himself to the "equal competition" syndrome so prevalent in his field—until he switched to another package, *tailored protection.*

"Mr. Russell," he says, after the opening amenities have been concluded, "I'm here to discuss our five-point tailored protection plan. This is a complete program we design on an individual basis for you and your family.

"This plan does five major things for you:

1. We help you get the kind of coverage *you* need, neither more nor less.

2. We help you keep your program up to date. We stay on top of your problems by getting in touch with you at regular intervals.

3. When insurance laws or practices change, we consult with you immediately to see what, if anything, must be done to maintain adequate coverage.

4. We help you in time of trouble.

5. We help you when you have a claim.

"Would you like to see just how this five-point protection plan would apply to you and your family, Mr. Russell?"

At this point, Kerr tells me, "I am no longer in the insurance business as such. Instead, I'm in the tailored protection business."

Having created this field on his own, Kerr enjoys a natural "monopoly" position. Granted, it's obvious when you come to think of it. The main thing is, it works. And while any salesman can do it, especially in the intangibles field where ideas, plans and programs play a heavy role, only those who actually do remove themselves from competitive comparisons can develop their own "monopoly" position.

Selling the Right Benefit Creates the Essential Difference

Another way of doing the same thing Kerr did is to sell a different benefit from those your competitors are plugging. Make sure, of course, that it's the one that will be of greatest value to your prospect—even if he doesn't recognize the fact right off.

Here, too, an example will best illustrate the point. The story begins when a meat packer called for bids on a large engineering job consisting of the design and supervision of installation of a meat preparation room, a meat storage room, and a freezer. The client firm stressed that price was the primary concern. Naturally enough, most of the consulting engineers concentrated on shaving their bids.

But one firm had its own ideas about this, for the prospect's specifications called for water cooled condensing units and blower coils in the meat preparation room.

"We knew this was wrong for the job," writes the senior consultant who was handling the negotiations for his firm. "Instead, we wrote in specifications calling for air cooled units and gravity coils. We explained that blower coils had proven unsatisfactory for other customers at the low temperatures required for this kind of installation. And employees complained about the cold air movement.

"In contrast to this, we included testimonials proving that gravity coils insured greater employee comfort and consistently better work output. Finally, we recommended that all units be installed outdoors, thereby allowing the firm to use the space allocated for a compressor room for other purposes.

"We sold this job to the customer at more than $3,000 above the lowest competitor bid for the design of the originally specified equipment."

"Why?"

"Because we convinced management that the real point was not the *cost* of the installation—but its *efficiency*. By sticking to the right benefit for the job, *we opened up a whole new ball game which put us in a completely different category from our competition.*"

2. RING IN THE OBVIOUS

Because as salesmen we are so close to our services, we often take one or another buy point for granted, not selling it as such in our customer contacts. It's so obvious to us, we forget it may be of real value to the customer—if only he knew about it.

You and your competitor may have "exactly equal" advantages and prices. But if you play up one of them when he doesn't, it becomes a difference from the prospect's point of view. And that's the view that overlooks the dotted line.

Selling the Procedure as a Difference

· Insurance adjusters, for example, all follow the same operating procedures—so obvious to all who sell the service that they universally ignore it. Or they did, until Roger Blackman came along.

Like his fellow salesmen in the field, Blackman always stresses speed of adjustment. "Everyone else makes the same claim," the prospect invariably retorts.

But where his competitors shrugged this off, Blackman met the implied brush-off head on. "That's exactly the point," he would exclaim triumphantly. *"We* can make good on this claim because our *operational control system guarantees it.*

"I've got to send in a daily report to my supervisor. *If I can't make a 24-hour contact or 48-hour inspection, I must let the supervisor know—and he must put someone else on the case. If necessary, he can pull people in from adjacent regions. This procedure is tightly controlled.*

"Why don't you give it a try and see for yourself?"

The italicized phrases describe a system of operation common to all Blackman's competitors. But he began to tip an increasing percentage of sales in his own direction because he capitalized on it as a buy point.

The conclusion is obvious: It's not a benefit until it's sold as one. If only you use it, the obvious benefit has been converted into a real difference.

3. YOU'RE PART OF THE PACKAGE

Salesmen often forget that one of the biggest benefits they can offer a prospect is the value of their own constructive thinking and services. When you need that extra benefit to clinch a deal, just remember—you're part of the package!

That thought takes us once again into the realm of the constructive call. Your personal ideas, your intimate knowledge of your plan and its applications to the prospect's needs, might well be the difference that pulls in the business.

Letting the Computer Do It

Your constructive contribution might be as simple as a personal follow-through after the sale to check on customer satisfaction. Or where the size of the sale so warrants, creating more elaborate difference may well be justified.

In one case, a top national corporation was in the market for a computer which was to be used in making the most rational allocations for its various operations. While competing representatives were busily discussing set-up costs, programming, etc., our man took the time to look around the prospect's New York offices. Among other things, he found that the firm had 36 file cabinets in 12 locations. Ten clerks handled the files as one part of their regular duties.

Using his firm's computer, this sales engineer figured out a plan for centralizing the files. This cut the number of cabinets from 36 to 20; enabled one person to handle the filing alone; and cut the volume of paperwork by nearly 40%.

Management was so impressed with this extra service—and with the demonstrated versatility of the computer—that the salesman's firm eventually got the order on the president's strong recommendation to the board.

There's no doubt about it. The constructive approach *you* dream up is truly unique. Thus you create a difference no competitor can match.

Not that your difference creating action or plan need be directly related to your services. In one case, the representative of a large financing organization felt sure that one prospect's sales personnel would benefit from more training in the selling of time-payment contracts.

At a luncheon meeting he arranged with the prospect, he outlined the idea of a training program to help the sales force sell "add on" purchases. He showed how they could be helped to introduce the subject of installment buying more successfully, how they could learn to do an even better job of servicing their more difficult customers, and how this improved salesmanship might well build application volume.

Taken with this idea, the prospect followed through with a program conducted by a sales consultant. The prospect's sales shot up sharply—and the salesman had a lucrative new account.

The salesman who contributes to his prospect's well-being in some such fashion does more than create a benefit difference. At the same time, he creates a competitive advantage for himself.

D. WRAP UP EACH MAJOR BUY POINT

Sometimes we make the mistake of assuming the prospect absorbs and accepts each point we make because he nods and says "yes." Ask for the order, however, and the "yes" can quickly convert to "no."

Why?

Because no matter how alert he may be, a buyer will at times get no more than a vague impression of your story the first time round—especially if your proposition is new or highly technical. But he may still "yes" you just to get rid of you faster.

Obviously, spelling out a benefit means very little in clinching a sale unless your prospect agrees to and understands it. You need a way of assuring that each important selling point actually "takes."

That's where your wrap up queries come in. To avoid being suckered by the "yes, yes" fallacy, you follow a two-step procedure.

    1. Focus the prospect's attention on but one major benefit at a time—polishing it until it shines.

    2. Taking nothing for granted, you qualify him, testing his understanding and acceptance of each major point *before you proceed to the next.* If his answer shows he has grasped the point and agrees to it, you move on to the next one. Otherwise, you backtrack, repeating the benefit in different words—then checking him out on it again.

Simple, isn't it? Yet experience shows you can't do a good job of it unless you work out your qualifying queries beforehand.

How One Man Does It

Let's look over the shoulder of banker Bruce Rozelle as he prepares to call on a well-established insurance office in connection with an Agent Plan his bank is promoting. Rozelle will be running up against stiff competition from finance companies as well as from other banks.

He starts the same way as in drawing up a "benefits brief," except that he doesn't use file cards. Instead, he draws a line down the middle of a sheet of paper, dividing it in two.

On the left hand side he lists all the major selling points he wants to get across to this prospect. Alongside each, in the right hand column, he writes out his qualifying queries. Like this:

BENEFITS	QUALIFYING QUERIES
1. The plan limits the possibility of a dealer's sidetracking you.	How do you think this might affect the chance of a dealer's putting a customer's financing and insurance in one package?

2. When you take the trouble to arrange his financing, your customer feels you put his interests first.

Some agents find that they build better customer relations when they arrange the financing. What has been your experience?

3. You open up other insurance possibilities: the full term insurance for the life of the loan and accident coverage, too.

I wonder what you think of the chances of adding accident coverage for the life of the term as an optional extra?

4. We furnish supplies and mailing pieces to aid you in your sales program.

Don't you agree that this promotional help in itself adds a substantial plus to our plan—which warrants your signing up for it?

A Matter of Finesse

Well-planned qualifying queries have a powerful cumulative impact. As the prospect *actively* assents to each point, his mind is geared to saying "yes" to the next. Slowly but surely, this builds a strong closing foundation. (More on this in the next chapter.)

But no prospect likes to feel that he is being played like a fish. Hit him once too often with a yes-inducing query—"don't you agree that . . . " and you'll lose him for good.

Now turn back to banker Rozelle's queries and see how he avoids this potentially dangerous fault. While he wants agreement, he shies away from reaching for it the easy way. Instead, he lets the prospect work it through himself with questions like: "How do you think this might affect . . ." and "What has been your experience?"

A series of agreements from such thought provoking queries will be far more meaningful than a flock of mechanical "yesses." What's more, this kind of question avoids the "yes, yes" misunderstanding. For the prospect can't answer it unless he really has been following you.

Note that Rozelle does cast his closing question in yes-or-no form. For at this point he wants to induce a favorable response to his application blank.

One thing would strengthen Rozelle's wrap up preparations. He should plan at least *two* qualifying queries for each buy point. That way, if he doesn't get acceptance on his first try, he can put it to the test again in different words.

When You Can't Gain Acceptance

That raises an additional point. Sometimes, despite an excellent presentation, the prospect remains non-committal even after a second check of his understanding or acceptance of a given benefit. What do you do then?

This is a matter of judgment. You might try a third time and be rewarded with a positive response. Conversely, the prospect may feel that you're willfully wasting his time if you persist after he has already brushed you off a couple of times. You just have to rely on your "feel" of each situation.

One thing is sure. You can't circle around any one point indefinitely. Move on gracefully when you must—leaving open the possibility of returning to the point later, if necessary.

You can do something like this: "I'm sure this will make more sense after we have explored some of the other features of this plan." Later, when you get his assent to some related point, you can then say: "Now that you've seen how this works, you might like to re-examine . . . ."

On the Telephone

On the telephone, as in face-to-face selling, the intelligent use of benefits plays a key role in increasing the percentage of sales to calls. Keeping a "benefits brief" handy is one way of doing it.

But no matter how detailed and descriptive your "brief," on the phone you still can't be sure that it's getting across—that your customer understands and accepts each major point. With no facial expressions to guide you, your best bet is to get a playback: to qualify him point by point as you go through your "brief." And here too, you'd best take the guesswork out of it by preparing your wrap-up queries beforehand.

Such qualifying queries serve another good purpose on the phone. For you make sure your customer *hears* you. He has to, in order to accept or reject the buy point.

Finally, on the phone more than in face-to-face selling, people resent listening to a monologue. Adroit wrap-up queries prepared to elicit more than a yes-or-no response provoke two-way discussion. And this mutual participation adds another intangible plus to the many factors that can make or break a sale.

IN A NUTSHELL

You'll move your prospects closer to the finish line when you put every major point in your presentation to the "benefit twins" test: Does it show the prospect what he specifically will save or gain when he buys?

You'll give yourself the best of it when you prepare a "benefits brief" *before* you call—punching each point home with pre-planned qualifying queries. From your "brief" you can pick and choose the right benefits for each call—those designed to make the man you're interviewing sit up and take notice.

Can your competitors match your offer? You'll gain an added competitive advantage by *creating* differences unique to you, preferably by the force of your own constructive ideas.

7

How to Handle Resistance
Constructively

New salesmen often fear the objections prospects may throw at them. The seasoned salesman welcomes such resistance. He knows that once he gets it into the open, he can come to grips with it constructively.

As one representative says: "Objections clue you in to the prospect's thoughts. Often they pinpoint the areas which interest him most—or least."

You can then build up the point or drop it, as the case may be.

Looking upon resistance as an opportunity helps you respond to it in a positive manner. You consider it carefully and answer it thoughtfully.

This attitude often communicates itself to your prospect. Because you take his feelings so seriously, he gives more consideration to your replies.

Digging Out Hidden Resistance

While most objections will be openly stated, some may remain hidden and unvoiced. This poses a problem. For how can you deal with unstated resistance?

Making matters worse, the prospect often conceals the hidden objection beneath a plausible sounding excuse. As J. P. Morgan once said: "A man generally has two reasons for doing things: one that sounds good—and the *real* one."

How can you tell the difference?

It's a matter of judgment and intuition. After years of experience, you get to sense when a stated objection is just a coverup for an unspoken one, or when a prospect is holding something back.

Since you can't cope with resistance unless you know what's causing it —you've got to cut through the surface pretense and probe to the real seat of the difficulty.

Ask a Leading Question—and Wait

Jack Crandall ran into this problem when he was selling a credit collection plan to a large retail merchant. The prospect listened intently to everything Crandall had to say and asked a number of intelligent questions.

Since he won acceptance on every major buy point, Crandall naturally assumed the man was ready to go ahead. Thus he was all the more taken back when his prospect said: "I don't know; I'll have to think it over."

Convinced there was something on the merchant's mind he didn't wish to express, Crandall decided to try the technique we were just discussing. "I see," he said calmly. "Is there any special problem that's bothering you, Mr. Meredith?"

Then he waited expectantly for an answer.

After hesitating for a couple of minutes, Mr. Meredith came out with it. It seems that he was worrying about how his customers would react when they learned he was turning their bills over to a collection agency.

Now that he knew what was wrong, Crandall dealt with the matter successfully. Had he been content to go along with the "I'll have to think it over" gambit, he might never have broken through to the sale.

Sometimes the surface objection may be valid enough. But if you are overready to accept it, you'll miss out on many a sale you could have made.

Once you're sure there is something below the surface, just nod in agreement with the stated reason and ask an appropriate leading question. Then let that pregnant pause go to work on your prospect. Often enough, this potent combination smokes out the hidden resistance.

If it doesn't work, you will have to fall back upon a direct attack. Say bluntly: "Mr. Manning, I sense that you have some objections to my proposal. What are they?"

One man who's tried it remarks: "You can't sell when they hold their cards to their chests. When nothing else works, this approach gets all the cards on the table—and gives you a chance."

Plow Around Him

Once you dig out the real objection or the prospect has aired it himself, you must still deal with it constructively.

The literature on selling abounds with suggestions on this score. A single chapter in one book on selling is headed: "81 Ways to Overcome Objections."

Actually, you don't need to memorize them all. For all these suggestions add up to one basic strategy: avoid a head-on clash. Trading punches might win the argument—but lose the sale.

Abraham Lincoln, who had a flair for dealing with people, applied this strategy instinctively. One day, after a particularly cantankerous visitor had gone, President Lincoln was asked, "How did you ever get that stubborn old codger to agree with you?"

"When I used to hold the plow," Lincoln replied, "and came to a very tough stump in the field, I never tried to rip it out. I just plowed around it. So with this man; I just plowed around him."

This basic strategy can be applied in many ways. But you'll do it most effectively when you concentrate on just a handful: the four techniques broad enough to cope with practically any resistance.

To handle resistance constructively, you should take into account each of the following pre-conditions:

    A. Prepare to meet anticipated resistance.

    B. Memorize the four basic how-to techniques:

        1. Agree with the prospect.

        2. Repeat the objection—in sharper terms.

        3. Treat the objection as a request for more information.

        4. Use a third-party witness.

    C. Consider your timing.

A. PREPARE TO MEET ANTICIPATED RESISTANCE

"Beat them to the punch," is as sound an adage in selling as it is in the prize ring. For an objection voiced by your prospect assumes more importance in his mind than one you've anticipated and disposed of before he gets to it.

There's just one caution. Anticipate the objection only when you're pretty sure it will be raised. Otherwise you may be creating an issue your prospect never thought of.

But where experience proves you can confidently expect a given objection, answer it first—and cut it down to size. And by so doing, you leave your mind free to cope with those forms of resistance which do not fall into some standardized category.

"Let Me Think It Over"

All too often the phrase "I'll think it over" kills a sale as the salesman stops selling today in the hope of landing the order tomorrow. In some cases, this may be the right thing to do. But generally, you'd best try to avoid such postponements—especially in the one-interview system.

Mind you, in answering an objection in advance, it doesn't follow that you state it in objection form. That is, you *don't* say: "Now, Mr. Smith, I know you would like to think about this plan for a while, but . . . ."

Rather, you present the case for immediate action as a positive advantage.

Sometimes this is fairly simple. If you are selling life insurance or some other form of protection, you can emphasize the need for locking the barn door while the locking's good.

Or you may have an inducement. "If you act today, Mr. Ashley, I am authorized to . . ."

In other cases, figuring out the best answer to anticipated resistance will not be easy. But where some powerful roadblock recurs time and again, it pays to look for some way of working into your presentation.

How To Do It

Regardless of the type of resistance you run up against regularly, you can best come to terms with it by applying the one-at-a-time method detailed in Chapter 2.

1. First list *your* recurring roadblocks. Include all which crop up often enough to warrant inclusion in your presentation.
2. Arrange them in the order of importance—with the one which most adversely affects your earnings rated #1, and so on.
3. Concentrate on the #1 objection long enough to register significant improvement.
4. When you have an approach that works and have built the habit of using it effectively, move on to #2 and focus on that. Continue in this fashion until you have covered every important recurring objection.

B. FOUR BASIC HOW-TO TECHNIQUES

When you answer an objection, you are in effect clashing with the prospect's views. One way or another, you must "plow around" the man, go along with his views, and then ease him into an appreciation of yours. Each one of the four techniques discussed here is simply another way of doing this effectively.

1. AGREE WITH THE PROSPECT

No prospect likes to feel he is being pushed. Nor does he relish an argument when he voices resistance. In most cases, you can put him in a more accommodating frame of mind by agreeing with him first. Then you yank his mind from preoccupation with resistance to contemplation of gain.

How?

By dissolving the objection in a strong solution of benefits. One good way is to follow up your agreement with a soft-sell query. "That's very true, Mr. Saks. However, I wonder if you've given any thought to . . . ?"

That's Exactly Why

You can sometimes heighten the impact of this strategy by converting the objection into the very reason for buying. That is, you not only agree, you actually appropriate the prospect's objection as your strongest selling point, as Pete Lasset did.

Pete was puffing some municipal bonds to a prospect who commented, "They sound good, but the yield is low."

"Of course," Pete replied.

(Pete's casual agreement creates the proper atmosphere.)

"But that's exactly why this investment makes sense for you," he continued. "Considering the growth stocks in your portfolio, these bonds give you what you most want now: unusual safety of your principal while earning a regular income for you which has the added advantage of being tax free."

Hugging his prospect's objection to his bosom, Pete gently draws the string by using it as his own best selling point. When the occasion warrants its use, the most formidable objections crumble before this approach.

2. REPEAT THE OBJECTION—IN SHARPER TERMS

When Richard Borden was Professor of Marketing at New York University, he arranged to tape record a variety of point-of-sale presentations. Together with his assistants, he recorded and analyzed thousands of real-life interviews.

One interesting fact emerged, among others. Those salesmen who repeated the buyers' objections *before* they answered them had a higher percentage of orders to presentations than those who neglected this practice. More significantly, *those who repeated the objections in even stronger terms, registered the highest percentage of all.*

Why does this technique carry so much weight? By repeating an objection in sharper terms, you have four things going for you.

1. You show you understand it—that you see the issue as your prospect does.
2. You demonstrate that you are not lightly brushing off his point of view.
3. When you restate his objection so strongly, your prospect assumes you have a good answer in reserve. This creates a "mental set" which makes a good reply sound better.
4. When played back so strongly, an objection may often sound exaggerated even to the man who raised it. Thus its importance is deflated before you come to terms with it.

"You Don't Care If You Lose Out?"

Here's how it works. The story begins when salesman Kenneth Diamond sweeps past a minor roadblock only to run headlong into a bigger one.

"I don't see how your system saves me money," his prospect objected as Kenneth concluded his opening promise.

"Maybe not. But do you write any of your business on a contingency basis?"

"Okay, I see what you're getting at and I guess you're right: you can reduce my loss ratios. But frankly, I don't care as long as my customers are happy."

"You mean you don't care if you lose out on your contingency as long as you build better relations with your customers?"

> (By rephrasing the objection so strongly, Kenneth primes the
> prospect for a strong reply and makes him retreat a bit).

"Well, I wouldn't put it quite like that, but my business does depend on good customer relations."

"Then let me ask you: when you tell your customer to send in his repair bill, doesn't he sometimes get a false idea of his coverage?"

"Yes, that's the part that bothers us. When the company denies liability, things can get rather embarrassing."

"That doesn't make your insured any happier, does it?"

The prospect shook his head.

"Now consider what happens when we handle your assignments. Just the other day . . ."

Because Kenneth's sharp restatement of the objection had deflated its importance in his own mind, the prospect listened intently as the salesman drove his point home with a case history.

There you have it. None of these resistance-handling techniques will guarantee the sale. But they should at least insure a full hearing.

And you always have a chance when they listen to your story.

An Exception

Up to this point, we've been dealing with objections which could be answered one way or another. But what if there's no good answer—as can happen upon occasion?

When faced with an unanswerable objection, *don't* linger over it. *Don't* repeat it; *don't* underline it in any way.

Do admit the truth of it, promptly and *briefly*—then turn the prospect's mind to thoughts of gain. Here again, soft-sell query will work wonders.

Let's watch salesman Gary Travers, as he steers his way past an unanswerable roadblock.

"Mr. Barnes, you've been sending in your big losses and claims for many years and we certainly appreciate it. But I notice that you never let us handle your smaller losses. Is there any special reason for this?"

> (With this leading question, Travers probes for hidden resistance).

"There sure is. I figure it's good public relations to handle small losses myself."

"That makes sense, But tell me: about how many small losses would

you say you handled personally last year—say those less than $100?"
"About 65."

> (Since Travers could hardly hope to convince Mr. Barnes that
> the personal touch was not good public relations, he admits the
> point casually, but does *not* repeat it. Instead, he moves the sale
> along with his first softsell query).

"Now it's been figured that an agent's time is worth $25 an hour when he's selling insurance. Let's say that in the time you saved by letting us handle those 65 loses, you could have sold just two or three extra policies. Would that be a reasonable estimate?"

"Yes, I suppose so."

"Then wouldn't it be a more productive use of your $25 hours?"

"Yes, but what about the cost of the service?"

> (Mr. Barnes' last question demonstrates that Travers' soft-sell
> queries have successfully focused the prospect's mind on the
> main point: selling more insurance and making more money.)

3. TREAT THE OBJECTION AS A REQUEST FOR MORE INFORMATION

Properly handled, the prospect's objections serve as a take-off point for closing the sale. Agreeing with him is one way of putting *him* in the proper frame of mind; repeating the objection strongly is another. To show your interest in his needs, mentally translate the objection into a question. Pretend he has asked for more information to explain why he should give you his business.

This puts *you* in the proper frame of mind for a constructive answer.

Responding to an offer from a financing company, one prospect remarked: "I can get better terms than that."

Instead of arguing the point, the salesman translated that to read: "What special feature does your plan have to justify its higher price?" Then he told him what those features were.

Too Much Red Tape

Objections stemming from customer complaints often respond well to this treatment. For example, a bank officer ran into that kind of situation when calling on a contractor who had closed out his account.

"Since your merger," complained the contractor, "there has been too much red tape. I used to be able to come in and say: 'Let me have $10 or $20,000,' and I'd get it. Now my requests have to go before a loan committee, I have to fill out a flock of forms, and then I still wait too long."

True, there had been a reorganization and the loan procedure had been tightened. Going into that, however, would hardly solve anything, the officer reasoned. Instead, he treated the objection as a request for more information.

"I see your point," he said carefully. "Basically, you want to know if you can still get a loan without fuss or delays. Is that right?"

"That's it exactly."

"Then I think I have the answer for you. Since you do need to borrow often, I suggest you establish a line of credit. That way, you can borrow up to that limit just as easily as you used to do—with no red tape at all."

The officer's constructive handling of the contractor's resistance, which like our other cases avoided the slightest feeling of disagreement, won back the account. Treating an objection as a request for information helps you build on what a man says—rather than tear it down.

4. USE A THIRD-PARTY WITNESS

Sometimes meeting resistance requires that you sharply oppose your prospect's views. To cushion the impact, you call upon an outside party to make the point for you.

Since you personally do not oppose the prospect, you avoid any chance of arousing hostility. Moreover, the prestige of the "witness" adds to the weight of your reply.

How It Works

To take one example of many, finance company salesmen who must compete against bank plans, as well as other finance companies, often run into a prospect who says: "I prefer to let banks discount my paper. They do a much better all around job than any finance company."

Now it's one thing to meet competition from another firm in your own field. While conceding the virtues of your competitor, you sell the differences, the advantages exclusive to you and your firm.

But where one class of business is pitted against another, you get a clash of views that can easily slide over the boundary separating discussion from argument. So if you can, you trot out a "witness" who will go to bat for you.

"Do you know Ray Bradley aown in Bloomfield? He runs the same kind of business as yours. Here's his phone number; he'll be glad to tell you why he prefers to deal with us. Why don't you call him now?"

Or you might have a letter from a satisfied customer referring directly to the point at issue. So you take it out of your bag and say, "You might like to see what a competitor of yours has to say on that score." Then show him the relevant paragraphs.

Better yet, if the prospect has the long-range potential to justify the trouble, you might arrange a face-to-face appointment with your witness. "Do you know Andy Hayes who runs the Buick agency on the other side of town? He'll be glad to talk to you about this personally, if we give him enough notice. Would you like me to arrange an appointment with him for sometime next week?"

A Caution

Make sure that you have the witness's okay *before* you quote him or refer a prospect to him.

A Matter of Choice

Which of the four ways of handling resistance is best for you? Agreeing with the prospect, can, of course, be combined with any of the others. As to the rest, it is a matter of choosing the technique which best suits your own temperament or which seems most appropriate to the given situation.

As one securities salesman points out: "What works on one man, may backfire on another. And what one salesman can work with, another one can't."

True. In your own case, trial and error practice will soon tell.

C. CONSIDER YOUR TIMING

When should an objection be answered? It depends.

Some You Answer In Advance

When you're sure that a particular objection will be raised by a prospect—or will be on his mind unvoiced—you answer it *before* it is raised by making it a part of your presentation. This minimizes it and gets it out of the way fast.

Most You Meet When Raised

As a general rule, you had best answer an objection when it is voiced. Otherwise, your prospect will keep chewing it over in his mind to the point that little else of what you say will sink in.

Some You Answer Later

Some presentations lose much of their bite when the cumulative effect of your prepared sequence is destroyed. Or you may feel that your answer will have greater impact after you have covered certain pertinent features.

In such cases, you can say: "That's a good point. I'll come to it in a moment."

But then be sure you do—and without too much delay.

A Few You Never Answer

Should you feel an objection is no more than an excuse for cutting you off and getting rid of you, ignore it and go on with your story. A case of selective deafness can be a valuable asset to a salesman upon occasion.

But *do* see such excuses as warning signals to pour on benefits that appeal specifically to this restless prospect.

IN A NUTSHELL

The experienced salesman welcomes resistance because he knows it will help him steer his way to the close. Each of the techniques of handling resistance is merely a variant of "plowing around the man": agreeing with him first—then leading him to an acceptance of your point of view.

Building the Habit

You have undoubtedly used some of these methods before. But as with all selling techniques, you will gain even more when you consciously build a *habit* of using one or more of them whenever the situation demands it.

BEFORE Each Call

From what you know of the prospect or customer, ask yourself if you can expect him to raise some specific objection. If so, work out an answer to it before you walk in. Even if it never comes up, knowing you're prepared will add to your air of confidence.

AFTER Each Call

Review the objections the prospect raised. What technique or techniques did you use to handle them? Did you choose the best one for each situation? Did you meet the resistance to *his* and *your* satisfaction?

If not, work out a more satisfactory answer for your next visit or for your next prospect. This before-and-after review will help you build the valuable habit of handling resistance constructively.

8

How to Close Successfully
in Intangibles Selling

You've been edging toward it from the moment you walked in on your prospect. You drew up plans for a constructive call, you worked out your opening strategy, you moved him further along the way with the help of the benefit twins, you turned his objections to your own advantage—all so that you could ease your prospect's mind closer and closer to the dotted line.

In short, you've primed him for action.

But all too many accounts are lost because a salesman stops selling precisely at that point. For no matter how convincing your presentation, *your job is unfinished until you ask for the order.*

Obvious? Perhaps. But the obvious has an unfortunate habit of being overlooked.

"You Never Asked Me."

There was the time Henry Ford told an insurance selling friend, "Jim, I just bought a new policy."

"Why didn't you get it from me?" Jim asked reproachfully.

Surprised, Mr. Ford replied, "You never asked me."

The Basic Strategy

"Asking," is the basic strategy. But the way you ask can strongly affect the ratio of sales to calls. And you can count on an even greater percentage of "yesses" if you take the trouble to hammer out a closing foundation first.

    A. Create a closing atmosphere.

    B. Ask for the order effectively.

A. CREATE A CLOSING ATMOSPHERE

Say you're selling paper towels or typewriters. You can show your product; demonstrate it in use; then quickly press for the order.

But selling intangibles is quite another matter. Without the solid substance of a tangible product, resistance stiffens. Because he can't see, feel, smell, or taste your service, the prospect will rarely respond to an overly quick closing attempt. Before he'll buy, he must thoroughly understand what you're offering.

One conclusion inevitably follows. The intangibles salesman who consistently creates a closing atmosphere as he moves the prospect along through each phase of the presentation is the man who will normally register the greatest number of sales. Adherence to four basic techniques will help produce this buy-minded aura.

1. Keep your order forms in sight.
2. Accentuate the positive.
3. Use motivating stories.
4. Keep testing for the close.

Let us examine each factor in turn.

1. KEEP YOUR ORDER FORM IN SIGHT

When getting ready for a presentation, there's one thing I invariably do first: I place my order form right on the prospect's desk. Mind you, I do so in a perfectly natural manner—without the slightest tinge of either apology or brashness. Never once has this stirred resentment.

A Two-Way Street

Several years back, I accompanied a friend of mine into the field for a few days. John did a fine job of *telling* his story; but when it came to *selling,* he was stymied by a marked inability to close. "John," I asked the second day out, "will you do me a special favor?"

"Sure."

"Then will you put your order form on the desk from now on at the same time as you pull out your presentation folder?"

John looked somewhat startled. But at the very next call he tried it, got himself a signed order, and has been flying high to this very day.

"I have been using this method ever since you suggested it," John writes, "and I am now batting .500. That's right, Abbott: I'm closing one sale out of every two interviews.

"I can't swear that having the order blank out does the trick exactly on its own. Nor can I tell you how it affects my prospects. All I know is that *it has a powerful effect on me:* making me wind up every presentation with a strong closing effort."

Here we get a glimpse of an important self-motivating factor. For creating a closing atmosphere is clearly a two-way street. Not only must the prospect be persuaded to buy, often the salesman must be persuaded to *ask*. Many a sale goes down the drain only because one or another psychological barrier inhibits a salesman from asking directly. As in John's case, putting your order form on the prospect's desk will work on *you* just as strongly as on the prospect.

2. ACCENTUATE THE POSITIVE

You'll more surely attain a buy-minded atmosphere when you take an affirmative stance early in the sale. Here again we have a double-barreled process. Presenting each major buy point in straightforward fashion is one side of the equation. Reaching for confirmation statements and decisions from your prospect is the other.

a. Make Positive Statements

Just one thing needs saying on this subject. In selling, no statement is a positive statement unless it comes wrapped in a promise of gain. Like this:

"Mr. Lansing, we have a plan which a good many men in situations like yours have been using to good advantage. I would like to discuss how we can adapt it to your needs."

b. Ask a Confirming Question

Since we have discussed this point at length under wrap-up of benefits, we need add only a few additional remarks. So long as unanswered objections remain in the prospect's mind, so long will the atmosphere be unpropitious for closing. Probing for confirmation of buy points with questions is one of the best ways of smoking out still-unvoiced resistance—thus opening the door for your buy-inducing response.

"Do you see how this plan will insure your son's college education?" Or, "Have I made clear how the 'automatic' feature of our plan keeps you posted all the time on cost of sales?" "Do you feel that your desire to add a few 'blue chip' stocks in your portfolio would be worth setting aside $40–$50 per month on the MIP program?"

A negative response to such confirming queries gives you your chance to strengthen your selling foundation. Conversely, every "yes" puts the prospect in a buying frame of mind. Indeed given a "yes" to a major query and many salesmen lead right into the close. "In that case, Mr. Brown . . ." and offer him an order form or application blank to sign.

OFFER A SERIES OF CONFIRMING CHOICES

A number of successful salesmen prefer a stronger variant: facing the prospect with a series of minor decisions, each of which adds one more brick to the closing foundation. Among tangibles salesmen, this is, perhaps, the most popular closing technique. "Shall we ship by railroad or truck?" or "Do you prefer the red or the black?"

With a little thought, the same approach can be adapted to the selling of intangibles. "Would a $10,000 policy tie in with your plans for the future, or would you prefer $15,000?" "Would you like our monthly Tax Record to be sent to your home or your office?"

In short, you make it simpler for your prospect to make the main buying decision by asking for a minor decision first. Actually, the great majority of sales can be seen as the culmination of a series of "minor sales." For as the customer says "yes" to your confirming questions and makes affirmative decisions to each minor choice you pose, he propels himself, step-by-step, to the final purchase.

As Charles B. Roth, author of "Secrets of Closing Sales" and many other books on selling, says "Give a *choice*, not a *chance*."

SOMETHING AGAINST SOMETHING

One experienced salesman adds an important postscript to this. "One thing will almost always improve the closing atmosphere: Offer something against something else when posing a minor choice, rather than something against nothing."

Again, the tangibles salesman enjoys an advantage in regard to the number of simple, "something against something" choices he can fall back upon. "Would you prefer our standard electric typewriter or our newest automatic model?"

While such choices do not come so easily for the intangibles man, they pay off well enough to warrant the time and thought that goes into their preparation. One bank officer, for example, has strengthened his closing efforts with such queries as: "Do you want your checks signed by the treasurer alone, or should they be countersigned?" "Would you like to pay off this loan in 12 months or would 18 months suit you best?"

As he concedes, these "something against something" choices do not in themselves finalize the sale. But each decision softens the prospect for the final one that does bring in the order. And that's precisely what creating a closing atmosphere means.

3. USE MOTIVATING STORIES

So much emphasis has been placed on the manner of asking for the order, that we often forget one truism: Few people will buy until they have been *motivated* to do so.

While how you ask does make a difference, as we shall see, you can't push a man into buying against his will. He must *want* to buy before your closing technique helps make him *your* customer.

That's why the top producers build the closing process around a motivating idea embodied in a real-life case history. Let's take one such sale from the point where the prospect has conceded a major advantage. "I must admit that what you say makes sense."

"In that case, don't you think *you owe it to yourself to let us* take some of the work load off your shoulders? Why just the other day . . ." and he's off and running with a motivating story which proves his case to the hilt.

(The italicized phrase is the claim, the motivating idea. The story seals and delivers it).

For the most part, motivating stories are cast in a positive mold. That is, they show how other individuals or firms have solved or prevented problems by doing business with you.

But in some situations, you'll get more mileage out of negative motivators: examples which show the harm people have suffered only because they did *not* use your services. One insurance agent who covers a number of small towns in the mid-west wins over many accounts against nationally advertised low-cost competition with the following story from his own files.

"Arthur Desmond," he says, "is a good client of mine who learned the hard way that insurance 'bargains' can cost too much. Several years ago he bought and remodeled an old home. Then he answered an ad which promised low premium insurance policies. When the company's out-of-town representative arrived, they quickly agreed upon the amount of insurance for both the home and its contents.

"As the years passed, he renewed his policy by mail. And he was quite happy with the savings this entailed—until a bad fire leveled his home.

"For the first time, he discovered he had been dangerously underinsured, even at the start. He was stunned when he received a check for less than half the value of his property. As costs continued to spiral, his insurance had become less and less adequate. He estimates that this inadequate protection cost him the fruits of more than nine of the best years of his life.

"Now he insures with us. As he puts it: 'With a local agent you get sound advice as well as a policy—and for only a few cents more.'

"Mr. Boyd, when you insure with us we inventory everything you own: the house, its contents, jewelry. We keep after you from time to time so that you add to it as you acquire new things and adjust your coverage accordingly. Wouldn't you like to enjoy the kind of on-the-spot coverage that puts your mind at ease?"

Against price competition, this kind of negative motivating story can swing many a sale which might otherwise be lost.

Build Your Own File of Motivating Stories

When you consider that no two closing situations are ever exactly the same, you can appreciate the need for an inexhaustible supply of motivating stories. The larger your fund of such stories, the more likely you are to come up with the one that turns the trick in a given case.

Remember John Heller? He's the man who made the Million Dollar Round Table with his 3x5 card file of back-up stories for his benefits briefs. The same system—indeed, some of the same stories—can work wonders here.

As with your "benefit-brief" back-ups, the best case histories are your own; those derived from your personal experience. The next best are those you pick up from other salesmen in your firm. You can build a collection of these by diligently swapping stories at sales meetings.

Nor should you neglect stories which apply to your field in general, those that often appear in trade publications. By telling these vividly—relating them to the *service* rather than to the competition—you can still gain the motivating impact you seek.

4. KEEP TESTING FOR THE CLOSE

In one sense, a trial close is every closing attempt you make aside from the one that lands the order. Here I use it more selectively to refer only to those closing attempts you make before you have formally completed your story.

Slipped into your presentation as early and as often as the situation warrants, the trial close serves you in four important ways.

1. *It keeps you from talking yourself out of your sale.*

Few prospects will buy unless your presentation creates a want. And this, as we have seen, generally takes longer for the intangibles salesman than for the man selling a tangible product. Yet I now suggest you try closing early and often.

Why the contradiction?

There isn't any.

Of course your prospect won't buy until he's properly motivated. But he may already be convinced before you start your story.

Perhaps an ad or a preapproach letter sold him. Maybe he's seen what your firm has done for someone else. Or a friend may have urged him to buy.

Then again, any one or combination of the buy points you dangle before him may sell him completely. In any such case, if you insist on running your presentation right through to the end, you may well talk him into a disastrous change of mind. For few things irritate a man more than a continuing sales message *after* he's decided to buy.

To avoid this danger, you send out a feeler: a trial close that tests your prospect's readiness to sign.

2. *When successful, the trial close saves the prospect's time—and yours.*

Every trial close that hits the jackpot—that sells without a complete presentation—leaves that much more time for another call.

3. *It helps expose weaknesses in your presentation which can then be readily repaired.*

A trial close shows you where you stand should you be losing your prospect. For his response will normally indicate if your presentation need be stepped up with a fuller exposition of benefits.

4. *They help break down the prospect's sales resistance.*

It's not that testing for the close will wear your man down. Rather, by working a trial close in on the heels of confirmed buy points, you rivet his attention to both sides of the equation: buy=gain. Gradually, this closing atmosphere gets under his skin.

If At First You Don't Succeed

Perry Miller, for example, was sure he had a sale sewed up when his prospect said: "Every businessman prefers more efficient methods."

Responding to this acceptance, Perry tested for the close. "When would you want the system installed?" he asked.

But the prospect retreated. "Oh no, it calls for too big an investment."

Alerted by this reply, Perry knew he had not yet fashioned a sufficiently strong foundation. His main selling point: the savings in time and money this card accounting system would effectuate, had evidently failed to get through to the prospect.

So Perry went over the ground again, this time more slowly and in greater detail. "Considering the savings in labor costs alone," he wound up, "don't you agree that this is an investment that will pay for itself in short enough time?"

"If your figures hold up, that could be true."

Again Perry made a trial close to capitalize on the prospect's confirming remark. And once again the latter held back. "I don't need to economize badly enough to warrant the initial investment."

Now Perry switched from present to future gains. "I realize, Mr. Hendricks that you don't need to economize today. But if things change and your business requires the savings our system guarantees—you may not have the capital to take advantage of it. In fact, in a tight money situation, you might be hard pressed to get the money you need to continue operations on your present basis. Am I right?"

When the prospect confirmed the validity of this statement, Perry swept into another closing attempt. "Then don't you think it makes sense to install this system *now* while you have the available margin? Maybe you don't have to save the labor costs on six employees now. But in bad times, that saving might be the difference between going under and riding out a storm. Do you agree with this reasoning, Mr. Hendricks?"

And this time the close worked. "I guess one has to take the long view," Mr. Hendricks affirmed.

Each Trial Gave Him a Clue

Twice the trial close had failed. But both times it served a useful purpose. The first test indicated that the main benefit had to be clarified if the sale was to go through. The second trial showed that present savings alone would not swing the business.

"Without that second clue," Perry admits, "I would never have gotten on to the right track: selling our system as 'bad times insurance.'"

Err on the High Side

How many trial closes should you make before you concede defeat? Circumstances will dictate. However, it is better to err on the side of too many than of too few.

As one salesman puts it: "You never know how close you are to the sale until you make the extra effort of trying for it."

The Matter of Timing

At what point in the sale should you make your first try?

There's no hard and fast rule. The answer will vary with the circumstances, the prospect, and the salesman's own temperament.

Some men start asking for the order in the same sentence in which they introduce themselves. Charles Williams, for example, opens up like this: "I'm Charles Williams of WDNB and I'm calling to invite you to enjoy the same returns our other advertisers have experienced."

As Williams says: "When I finish this introduction, I have my order book out and my pen poised. Then I pause for a full minute. So many prospects are already sold on advertising with us, this often gets the business. In a jiffy, I'm off on another call."

This is, of course, an extreme example. Most experienced salesmen adapt their trial closes to their prospect's reactions. Looking and listening carefully for the slightest "buying signal," they then come in smoothly with their testing query. (And don't forget the added touch of keeping your order form in sight.)

What Are Buying Signals?

When by action or word your prospect indicates he is coming close to a decision—that's a buying signal. It signifies: "Stop selling and start closing."

How do you recognize such signals?

After years in the field, many salesmen can sense such situations. But you need not rely on intuition. If you stay alert to what your prospect says and does, you can usually tell when he's ripe for a trial close.

For example, he may finger the order form you've left on his desk or start reading the fine print in your policy. Often, he'll betray himself by the questions he asks.

Buying signal questions will take many forms. "How much did you say this policy will pay me if I'm totally disabled?" or "Did I understand you to say that . . . ?" And so on.

With your prospect before you where you can watch the expression on his face and hear the tone of his voice, you can readily judge if questions like these are true buying signals. When you think they are—tack a trial close onto your answer.

Should his reactions show you misread the signs, you haven't lost a thing. On the contrary: for now you know you've got some more intensive *telling* to do.

The trial close is a powerful sales tool. When the buying signs are flashing green try one. You'll sell a lot more that way.

B. ASK FOR THE ORDER EFFECTIVELY

It's better to ask for the order bluntly than not to ask at all.

Still, the more skillfully you do it, the more sales you'll ring up. This does *not* mean playing tricks on the prospect. A man who feels he's been trapped into buying, will hardly remain as a lasting customer.

By skillful asking, I mean making the most of modern psychology and of the know-how successful salesmen in every field have accumulated over the years.

In this section, we shall focus on the four outstanding closing techniques:
1. Assume the sale.
2. Close on a buy point.
3. Weigh the pros and cons.
4. Ask for a piece of the business.

1. ASSUME THE SALE

Ty Cobb never worried about a catcher's throwing arm nor a baseman blocking his path. He simply assumed that more often than not he would beat the throw or bowl over the fielder.

Because of this faith in his own ability, he was off and running every chance he got. Sure, he was thrown out 39 times in his record breaking year. But nobody cares about the times he was caught.

All that matters are the 96 stolen bases he piled up.

Similarly, a simple faith in your firm and your presentation will help you pile up more sales. For when you assume the sale you never question the prospect's desire to buy. You just take it for granted that he *will* buy; that he'll buy from you; and that he'll do it now.

This lends you an air of assurance buyers respond to.

Sure, you'll be "thrown out" on occasion. But more often than not, resistance will melt away.

"I'm Ready to Take Your Order."

Consider the man who had been having a hard time getting his prospect to make up his mind on two previous calls. Reviewing these interviews, the salesman was struck with the number of advantages this prospect stood to gain by acting on the offer. "This hit me so forcibly," the salesman recalls, "that I phoned the man and made a luncheon appointment for the following day.

"Over our coffee, I reviewed the benefits he'd gain by doing business with us, just as I had done by myself. Then, in a completely casual manner, I said, 'Mr. Manfeed, I'm ready to take your order.'

"Just as casually, he replied, 'I guess we can do business.'

"Until that time I had always found closing the most difficult part of a call. But assuming the sale does the job so naturally, it has become by far the most productive technique for me."

True, this case may be somewhat unusual. Yet it does illustrate nicely the psychological factors involved.

For you can hardly take the sale so completely for granted unless you have absolute confidence in your firm and its services. This engenders an enthusiasm that can be highly contagious.

What's more, your prospect feels that your offer must be worth considering when you assume the sale so casually. That's why he'll ride along so often on the same psychological wave length.

One Caution

As in every part of your presentation, the closing techniques you apply should mesh with what you know of the prospect's personality. Some may object to anything that smacks of being presumptuous, no matter how reasonable it may seem to you.

Still, in most cases you can assume the sale without in the slightest degree taking away from the prospect his prerogative of making up his own mind. If you feel comfortable in using it, you'll bring in far more sales than you'll blow.

And remember. It's the ones you bring in that count.

2. CLOSE ON A BUY POINT

Some salesmen prefer a simple request. "Are you ready to do business, Mr. Claiborne?"

When a solid closing foundation has been laid, such a direct request will often produce results. However that may be, you'll do even better when you wrap your request around a major buy point.

Like this: "Don't you think you owe it to yourself *to let us take some of the work load off your shoulders* with our monthly analysis?"

Tie It On To Your Motivating Story

You'll give yourself the best of it when you tack your closing buy point to the end of a motivating story. Here's a case in point.

A bank officer was assigned to a distributing company which often shipped machinery to various cities, relying heavily on credit agencies for information. This gave the banker a clue for getting his foot in the door.

On his first call, he played up the information gathering facilities of the network of correspondent banks his own office was tied into. While somewhat impressed, the prospects did not quite see why this would be any improvement on the work of the national credit agency which had always done a good job for them.

Undaunted by this resistance, the banker threw one of his motivating stories into the breach. "After receiving a large order from a firm of architects," he said, "one of our customers drew a commercial credit report which showed a poor pay record and thin capitalization.

"When I heard about this, I checked with our local correspondent bank. This was a temporary situation, they informed me, due to the buy out of a partner. Previously, the firm had built an excellent credit record.

"Reassured by this information, our customer offered helpful terms and now has a fine account. Had they used only the commercial report, they tell me, their terms would have been either prepaid or C.O.D.—and the relationship would probably have been very brief."

Now the bank officer moved directly from his motivating story to his closing buy point. "Your commercial agency can perform a valuable service. But in some cases, this should be supplemented with more *up-to-date information* which our local correspondent banks can normally provide."

Results? The principals agreed to let the bank handle their next credit investigation assignment.

Of course, the situation could just as easily have been reversed. That is, a representative of a credit agency could use a buy point close to win a piece of the business from strongly entrenched bank competition.

And that's precisely the point. Most salesmen *know* the closing strategies discussed here. But the sales roll in to those who *apply* them consistently.

3. WEIGH THE PROS AND CONS

Now we come to the weightiest (no pun intended) closing technique. With hard-to-convince prospects, or thrown into the breach after previous attempts have failed, it often works wonders.

You've completed your presentation. All the ingredients for making the sale—or losing it—are out in the open. Yet your prospect won't commit himself, no matter how hard you try. To get him to move, you decide to add up all the reasons for and against buying, balancing the one against the other.

"Isn't it dangerous to bring up reasons *against* buying when you're trying to close?" some salesmen have asked.

Perhaps. But "hiding" the cons will help you just about as much as "hiding" his head in the sand helps an embattled ostrich.

For your prospect has all the negative factors on his mind anyhow. And you can be sure *he'll* weigh the disadvantages against the advantages before he'll buy.

Then why not beat him to the punch?

When you candidly add up the pros and cons yourself, you keep the weighing process in your own hands. Surely, you'll be fairer to your offering than your prospect would be.

At the same time, the weighing process eats away at the barrier of suspicion that generally surrounds the difficult prospect. For in effect you're saying: "I've put all my cards on the table. You've seen the bad side; you've seen the good. Now you know from the weight of all the evidence, that you have more and stronger reasons for buying than for turning me down."

That's a difficult argument to shrug off.

How One Man Does It

Fred Bascomb sells independent merchants the idea of associating in a voluntary chain with other independent retailers. "Boy," he says with a grin, "some of these merchants are the toughest babies in the world to sell.

"The plan is really good. But you've got to pound some of these men over the head with a hammer before they'll move. I've tried every closing technique in the book; however, I get my best results when I close with the pros and cons.

"Not too long ago, for example, one man in Pasadena gave me a pretty rough time. No matter what I said, he didn't like our plan; he didn't need it, he didn't want it, and he wouldn't buy it.

"Finally, I took my belt in a notch or two and gave it all I had. 'Look Mr. Martineau,' I said, 'we'll never get anywhere this way. Let's weigh the pros and cons of this deal and then decide. Here's my pen: you add up each point yourself.' "

(The last two sentences are gems of psychological selling. That "Let's weigh," immediately sets a tone of mutual participation. Then giving him the pen and inviting him to "add up each point yourself," made the prospect feel that *he* and not Fred was doing the deciding).

"Let's consider the disadvantages first," Fred went on. "You're hesitant about this move for three reasons, basically. To begin with, as you pointed out, you'll be paying for something intangible. You get nothing you can resell at a profit.

"Second, you must submerge your identity by taking on a chain name. And finally, you'll no longer be as fully independent in making decisions as you've been before. Have I stated the case fairly, Mr. Martineau?"

"Yes, you've got it straight."

"Is there anything else you have against the idea?"

(By adding this question, you demonstrate that you're not trying to hold back on any negative aspects.)

"No," said the prospect. "But those are enough."

"We'll see. Let's consider the pro side now. You've agreed that you get much larger buying power—with all the savings that entails. Can we put that down as a plus?"

(When weighing your pros and cons it makes good sense to get confirmation on every point).

"Yes, that's fair enough."

"Still on the pro side," Fred continued, "you yourself recognized that the syndicated advertising service you get will cut your promotion costs and increase your store traffic."

(You heighten the impact when you can remind the prospect that he himself had previously confirmed the point you are now adding to the pro side of the scales.)

"On top of that, you get headquarters help with your planning and display. With a more attractive store, don't you agree that you'll have a better chance of keeping the extra customers our advertising brings in?"

Mr. Martineau nodded.

"But help in buying and selling isn't the whole story, by any means. Since you'll be keyed in to our headquarters accounting section, you also get an improved control system.

"Now, Mr. Martineau, you've weighed the pros and cons yourself. When you come right down to it, our plan adds up to one basic advantage: It lets you compete on more equal terms with the two giant chains right here in your neighborhood.

"Do you think you should go even one more day without the help our group can give you?"

"Mr. Martineau thought that one over for several minutes," Fred reports. "He joined, all right."

Give Yourself the Best Of It

While you don't want to hold back any minuses—you'll undermine your presentation if you do—there's no reason why you shouldn't give yourself the best of it. You do so by the manner in which you handle the weighing process.

    a. Chalk up the minuses *first*. That way, the prospect gets the full impact of the plus factors just before your closing appeal.

    b. Present the pros in the form of benefits. Fred Bascomb did this beautifully. "You get this, which means thus and so; you get that, which brings in the other; etc."

As Fred himself concludes: "The pros and cons technique gives you plenty of room to maneuver. As you sum up, you can reinforce whatever selling points struck home the first time round, you can ring in new ones you overlooked before and you can directly counter the prospect's strongest objections. If I had to throw out every closing device but one, this is the one I'd hang on to. It has a dramatic force that often sells when everything else has failed."

4. ASK FOR A PIECE OF THE BUSINESS

In many intangible fields, the salesman must compete quite often against lines that give equal service at the same price. How can these men get business away from competitive firms?

One good answer, as we saw in Chapter 6, is to sell the differences embodied in your own constructive service as a salesman. Another is to ask for a small portion of the business as a starter.

Probably the best way to justify that request, is to use stories with negative motivation. Emphasize the wisdom of having a second company to fall back upon in an emergency. Then underline the point with a grim tale of losses incurred when a serving company was unable to meet the client's needs because of a strike, an accident or a natural disaster.

Getting a Foot in the Door

In one case, the president of a growing firm turned down a closing effort in the way many salesmen find so discouraging. "Frankly, we see no need for additional help. Our present serving company has been very flexible in adjusting itself to our needs."

But the salesman was Jens Jensen of Houston who has evolved a method of handling such situations after long experience. "Of course," Jens replied. "United offers extremely fine service. Naturally you want to continue doing business with them."

That casual "of course," combined with repeating the objection, set the proper tone for Jens' second closing attempt which, this time, came on the heels of a negative motivating story.

"But have you ever considered what might happen when you need someone else in a hurry? It's not so easy to find someone who knows your problems and is familiar with your methods of shipment. Besides, without an established second-line relationship, you can't always be accommodated when you need it. May I tell you of one such case?"

"Go right ahead," said the president. "I'd like to know."

"Some time ago," Jens went on, "I faced a similar situation with a firm which had equally strong ties to its freight forwarder. As in your case, they saw no need of a second connection.

"But they called on us for help when our competitor was closed down by a strike. Unfortunately, we were committed to other firms which had been giving us some of their business all along. So this outfit suffered a bit of a loss before it could get its shipments untangled. Don't you think they would have been wiser to have prepared for any contingency *before* the event?"

(As always, an experienced salesman reaches for a confirming statement before pressing on to his close.)

"I guess you're right."

"In that case, Mr. Farley, why not let us handle some of your business now? That way, you can see the kind of service we can give you and you'll know you can count on us when the going is rough."

Mr. Farley capitulated.

"By prefacing my bid for part of the business with this negative all-the-eggs-in-one-basket story," Jens reports, "I now get some assignments in situations where I used to get a total rejection. Once we get our foot in the door, we can often pave the way to an increasing share of the business."

Whether your taste turns to negative or positive appeals, the principle remains the same. When competing against entrenched relationships, angling for a portion of the business is often the better part of valor.

Commit Your Prospect to Action

The sale does not necessarily end when the prospect says "yes." For at times you must still contend with a psychological "law of inertia."

In nature, this law tells us, bodies at rest tend to stay at rest. Thus you must expend a well-calculated spurt of energy to get them moving.

So it is in selling. Even after the prospect agrees that your offer makes sense, you've got to prod him into immediate action.

Many intangibles salesmen have recourse to the dotted lines on their order forms. Those who are not so blessed, must commit their prospects to specific *verbal* activity.

"Fine; you agree that we should do business. When shall we start?"

The moment he places a date on it, you can be sure of the sale. Mind you, I'm *not* talking about legalisms or trust. I'm just concerned with the psychology of assuring that your prospect stays sold by inducing him to commit himself one way or another.

The bigger your supply of mental prodders, the better. "Which building do you want us to start servicing?" or "Where should I make my first pick up?"

Questions like these will help you move the mind at rest.

IN A NUTSHELL

Effective closing can be summed up in exactly 9 words: Assume the sale—and always ask for the business.

BUILDING THE HABIT

Before You Call

Do you have enough motivating stories and minor choice queries to help create a closing atmosphere? Are you mentally geared to place your order form on the prospect's desk and to keep testing for the close at every opportunity?

Do you know enough about your prospect's needs to confidently assume that he does require your services? Have you sufficient ammunition to make a pros and cons closing, if need be?

Self-questioning in this manner will help develop the habit of preparing yourself for strong closing efforts in every interview.

After You Call

If you didn't make the sale, do you know why? Could you have built a more effective closing foundation? Should you have slipped more trial closes into your presentation? How did you ask for the order? Could you have done it better? Would a different method have helped?

Such after-the-call reviews will help you select and refine those closing techniques which best suit your temperament.

PART IV

Keeping Your Intangibles
Customers Sold

9

How to Keep the Sales Door Open
Through the Customer-Oriented
Approach

In the two-interview system, you design the first call as an exploratory, seed-planting conference. To make the sale, you must keep the door open for your return.

In many intangibles fields, however, the salesman always walks in for a do-or-die effort, attempting to close on the very first call. If he doesn't make the sale, he may or may not aim at a second try—depending on the kind of service he's selling and on his company policy.

Some firms insist that a second try isn't worth the candle. Yet in most fields the evidence shows that more sales are closed on a second selling try to the same prospect than on the first. From the creative standpoint, an unsuccessful first call can at least get you closer to the prospect's problems. While I have always preferred to move slowly to the sale, I recognize the validity of the one-interview system in some situations—and businesses. Whatever the policy, common sense as well as creativity dictates a modicum of flexibility. Surely, if the long range potential is high, a rule can occasionally be bent to the advantage of all concerned.

How, then, can a one-interview salesman get the welcome mat out for a second call once he's been turned down, but feels that there is a reasonable certainty of a second call sale? Although the details may vary to fit the system being followed, the basic strategy remains the same. For best results, when faced with a final "no," convert momentarily to a two-interview operation, especially when you feel certain that a second contact will do the job.

A Matter of Definition

Before going into the how of it, let's define our terms. In some cases, an exploratory effort may extend over two or more interviews. Indeed a growing number of firms expect salesmen to conduct several fact-finding interviews before making any attempt to close.

To simplify matters, I shall lump *all* exploratory calls under the one heading: "first interview." Only the strictly selling call will be classified as "second" or "subsequent interview."

Of course, in the one-interview system *all* calls are (or should be) a creative combination of fact-finding and selling.

A. HOW TO SELL YOURSELF INTO A SECOND INTERVIEW

You'll line up more second selling interviews when you follow this proven 3-step process:

1. Explain why you will be back—and do it constructively.
2. Close the sale: *ask for a specific appointment.*
3. Follow through.

Actually, each step plays a dual role. For one, it serves the essential keep-the-door-open purpose. At the same time, each helps build a closing foundation under the impending interview.

Let us analyze each step in turn:

Step 1. Explain Why You Will Be Back—and Do It Constructively

If your exploratory call proceeds as planned, you've demonstrated your concern for the prospect by helping him bring *his* needs and problems into the open. In angling for the second selling interview, keep your eye—and his—on the same ball. More often than not, he'll *want* to hear your proposal once you make clear that the second call will be built around a solution suggested by the first—"What I have learned today, Mr. Rambo, makes it possible for me to do a good job for you," and so forth.

Most people will respond more readily to a made-to-measure solution. Real estate salesman Randolph Wyatt chalks up a goodly number of second interviews something like this: "Now that you and your wife have clarified your situation, Mr. Andrews, I think I can prepare a sound property investment plan for your consideration. *Of course I need time to work it out in a way that will do the best possible job for you.* As soon as I'm ready, I'll ask for an opportunity to discuss it with you in detail."

Personalizing the need for a second interview with a business prospect may require somewhat more finesse. For one thing, he knows you'll often need more information as well as more time to individualize the plan. So let him know you intend to get it. As Lawrence Paisley does.

Paisley, who does a good job of selling the services of a management consultant firm, reminds his prospect that "all our services are tailored to the special circumstances and need of each client. That's why we must investigate your position in the industry further *before we can be sure of doing a thorough job on your behalf.* When I come back, *I will be ready to discuss a plan that will meet your needs."*

MAKE IT AS SPECIFIC AS POSSIBLE

The more clearly the problem has been defined, the more clearly you can explain what you propose to do in the second interview. And the better you'll be for it.

"Could I call you for an appointment when I'm ready with a complete plan for guaranteeing your grandson's tuition?"

"Now that I know what you have in mind, Mr. Raines, I'd like to come back with a plan that will help you build up virtually tax-free funds and permit your corporation to pay your estate taxes for you at a discount upon death."

When the Prospect Says "No"

On the face of it, one-interview-system salesmen have a tougher job on their hands. When the prospect has just turned them down after listening to their proposition, a second visit would seem to promise little more than a repetition of the same.

Then why not convert right then to a two-interview method for that sale? But as I've said before—*only* when you feel *sure* there is a sale to be made. That is, act as though you have just completed a fact-finding interview and want to return with a personalized presentation.

Since in most cases the interview *will* have given you a good picture of the prospect's needs, just a little twist may suffice to put you in the same position as a two-interview man. Like this:

"Mr. Mandel, I can see that what I came prepared to talk about today is not what your particular situation requires. *However, now that you have clarified the situation for me, I'd like to work out a plan with your particular needs in mind.* I should be ready in about a week and will give you a ring at that time."

DROP A QUESTION INTO THE SLOT

The "no" is conclusive; the potential is there—but suppose you still don't have a clue to the prospect's real interests. What do you do then?

What you should have done in the first place: ask him—directly or indirectly as the case may be. Then you keep the door open for a second try, exactly as indicated above: "Now that you have clarified . . ."

BRING IN A SPECIALIST

When your doctor tells you he'd like to discuss your case with a specialist, you may feel worried. But you'll probably appreciate his concern—and look forward to hearing the suggested course of action.

The same can hold true for certain other intangible services. If the sale has fizzled, you can sometimes keep the door open for a second try by explaining that you'd like to consult a specialist.

Securities salesman Harold Wolfe tells me this ploy has worked for him on a number of occasions where he felt a call-back was warranted. "Look," he will tell the prospect, "why don't we leave the matter open for a week or so. *I'd like to discuss your specific problem with the manager of our mutual funds department.* With his help I'm sure I can come back with the kind of balanced program you were talking about."

Mind you, the man has refused Wolfe's offer. Yet in more than half such cases, Harold says, this let-me-consult-a-specialist approach racks up a second interview.

SUGGEST A TRIAL

A salesman for an insurance adjustment bureau swears by this method of securing a second interview after a firm turn down. "Let me make a proposal," he says. "You've never tried our service, so how about giving us the first three casualty claims that come into your office in each of the next two months?"

"That way, *you* can be the judge. If it works out the way I've said it will, we can discuss the matter further when I return."

"Fair enough," many an agent replies. "I'll give it a try."

None of this is to say that as a one-interview salesman you should not try again and again in the first interview. Actually, unless you are revoltingly high pressure the first time, your chances of making the sale the second time around will surely be greater if you have asked for the order one or more times in the first interview. People expect salesmen to *sell!*

Step 2. Close the Sale: Ask For a Specific Appointment

Remember the one unshakeable rule in selling: ask for the order. True, in the two-interview system, the first call is exploratory. But while you're not selling the service—*you are constantly selling the second interview.*

Getting the order in this case means winding up with a specific appointment for your return.

In most of the examples above, the salesmen kept the selling interview open-ended. "I'll call you when the plan is ready." "Preparing a plan should take a week or so."

This does have the virtue of underlining the time and effort you'll be pouring into a constructive proposal slanted directly at the prospect's needs. But it's *not* the best way of doing it.

From past experience you'll generally know just about when your proposal will be ready. Pinpoint the *day* and *time* and you'll impress your prospect with your confidence and ability to do the job for him. More to the point, when he puts that second interview down on his appointment calendar, you've made your first big move toward landing the sale.

Give Him a Choice

With that thought in mind, you can use the appropriate closing techniques. "Mr. Jensen, I'll be ready to be back in this neighborhood on Wednesday, March 17 with a plan to meet your expansion needs. Will the morning or afternoon be more convenient for you?"

"Wednesday morning is usually a slow time for me."

"Fine. What about 10 o'clock, then—or would you rather make it closer to noon?"

"Let me put it down for 10."

Suggest a Quiet Place

If it's a big sale and dependent on a complete and uninterrupted presentation, you might want to secure yourself against this problem. Perhaps a lunch or dinner date away from his office would be best. Or you might ask the prospect to arrange this as a private, no-interruption conference. A good salesman never hesitates to ask a prospect to shut off calls during an interview. Prospects respect you for asking this courtesy.

One successful salesman of group insurance refuses to operate in any other fashion. "When I come back with a presentation," he says, "I've got a lot of time and effort invested in it. Well, I won't make that investment unless I've got an appointment lined up and the prospect's assurance that neither visitors nor phone calls will come through. And let me tell you, they respect me for it."

Make It a Third-Party Appointment

The "Third Party" gambit is akin to the technique of explaining to the prospect that you want to come back after consulting with a specialist. This time, you arrange for him to meet with both you and the specialist.

Consider the bank officer who was having a tough job of making his prospect hold still for a second interview to discuss an Estate Plan. "Mr. Moore," he said finally, "I know you feel that you have already made sound arrangements for the administration of your estate. But if our senior trust officer could personally assure you that every possible pitfall has been accounted for—would that give you greater peace of mind?"

"I guess it would, at that."

"Since you see it that way," the officer said, "I would like you to come in and meet our Mr. Raymond. If Friday morning would be convenient for you, I believe I can arrange an appointment right now."

"Would he be free at 9:30?"

Like so many before—and after—him, the reluctant Mr. Moore found it hard to walk away from an appointment with an expert—for free.

Thrown in as a last resort, the same technique helps a one-interview insurance salesman revive interest after a turn down. This man keeps "one of our company lawyers" in reserve for high potential prospects. "If you'll let me fill him in on your problems, I can bring him back here *at no expense to you* a week from Wednesday—that's the 23rd. By thrashing it out together, I'm sure we can eliminate the tax drain that's been bothering you."

Nor does the idea have to be limited to providing free expertise. For example, when real estate salesman Sam Harris broached the idea of a branch store at a new shopping center to the proprietor of a specialty food shop, the prospect balked at the size of the indicated capital investment. And he waved aside every effort to set up a further discussion of the matter.

At least, he did until Harris asked: "Would you like to meet a man with a broad experience in the food field—and who will consider investment?"

True, you can't pluck such helpful third parties out of your hat. But an alert salesman can have an expert or two, a would-be investor, an idea man, or whatever on tap for that odd occasion when a big sale looms. Then if need be, he can bring this third party into the breach as an appointment-clincher.

Step 3. Follow Through

Drop the prospect a line or phone him a day or so in advance of the second meeting to reconfirm the appointment and remind him of its constructive nature. Treat this follow-through as you would the pre-approach to a first interview.

That is, *don't* try to sell. *Do* emphasize the fact that the call will center around *his* interests.

"Two sentences will do the trick," says one man whose sales record proves the point. Phoning (never more than two days in advance), he tells the prospect: "I just wanted to let you know that we've worked out a proposal *along the lines you suggested last time.* I'll be in at 2:30 on Tuesday as we arranged."

A Delayed Try

In this connection, when some one-interview salesmen feel sure of a second-call sale, they use a follow through contact as a delayed attempt at gaining a meaningful second interview. If the atmosphere seems too charged immediately after the turndown or if they have no good ideas at the time they make no keep-the-door open effort on the spot.

Instead, they phone or send a letter a few days later to inform the prospect that after some thought (or further investigation, or discussion with the home office, or whatever) they now have a suggestion which will be closer to the prospect's needs as revealed in the first interview. Then they press for a second appointment.

Of course, this method can also be used if an initial face-to-face try for a second interview has failed. And it works often enough to warrant the effort.

B. HOW TO PLAN THE SECOND INTERVIEW

If you slot your initial calls as fact-finding expeditions, you must reckon with the prospect's expectations when you return to press for the sale.

Consider. Your exploratory interview focused on *his* facts: his needs and problems. He'll surely be looking for a proposition that does more of the same. Let him down and you'll be working against heavy odds.

If anything, this goes double for the one-interview salesman. For in effect, by maneuvering for a second shot after a "no," you've made a promise.

"Okay, you've turned down my offer. But if you allow me to make a second presentation, I'll be back with an offer that's right up your alley."

The moral? Whichever system you follow, you'd best prepare a truly constructive call. Then the odds will be tilting your way.

You'll make the most of your second interview when you follow the 4-point procedure:
1. Remind him why you're there—briefly.
2. Repeat and reconfirm every basic agreement.
3. Keep it constructive.
4. Ask for the order.

1. Remind Him Why You're There—Briefly

Remember: your prospect expects you to pop up with an idea, a plan, a service designed to ease or solve his problems. If you want him to listen, let him know you've come through.

But *do* make it brief. For your sale will turn on the cumulative impact of what went before plus what you've got now.

"Mr. Banks," you might say, "I've got a proposal mapped out which meets every point you raised last time. But let's hold the details for a moment."

Then head straight for the flashback. That takes us to our second point.

2. Repeat and Reconfirm Every Basic Agreement

In any presentation, the professional salesman will backtrack after an interruption. That is, *he repeats what he was saying,* before moving on to the next point.

Why?

Because he knows that a successful close rests *not* on any one buy point but on the cumulative force of the entire presentation. To harness that force, he must get the prospect's mind back in the groove.

When you walk in for your second interview there's been a longer break. Your proposal won't hit home unless you lead him back into your selling track first.

In short, the greater the time lapse, the greater the need to review and reconfirm the basic points of the previous interview. Jim Barnett has built an enviable record using the two-interview system, closing six out of ten second-interview calls.

"*Before* I walk in, I have selected all the major points on which my prospect *agreed* in the first interview. First, I tell him that I think my plan for him now conforms to the issues as *he* saw them the first time. Then I ask if we can go into them later. Normally he says 'yes.'

"Now I take him through each of the major points I selected and one by one I *reconfirm his agreement* on them.

"This serves two purposes. First, it puts him into an affirmative state of mind. Secondly, it gets him into the act. The more he gets involved, the more he feels that he and I are working together to help *him* with *his* problem.

"If I do this well, the rest of it is easy sledding. For each part of my proposal follows logically on the points he himself has ticked off."

Make No Exceptions

Despite all the evidence to the contrary—and Barnett's is merely one of many success stories—making a second selling presentation poses a problem to some salesmen who try always to operate on a one-interview basis. They fear the prospect will find the story dull on a second hearing.

But the backtracking rule on interruptions is based on the average prospect's short memory span for any sales message. At home or in the office, the prospect is thinking about *his* chores, his troubles—not yours. Given the normal sales resistance triggered by your very presence, he is easily distracted, your message easily blotted from his mind. Indeed, he may never have absorbed it the first time round. Obviously, it didn't register enough the first time, or he would have bought.

Making him remember is not your first *worry,* it's your first *job.* Yet curiously enough, you've got one psychological factor going for you here.

For while he doesn't remember *consciously,* you do reinforce his *unconscious* as you review and reconfirm.

How Long Should It Be?

"How long should the review take?" some salesmen have asked.

There's only one general rule: just long enough to prime the prospect for your revised and polished proposal. This can vary widely with the circumstances.

Just a couple of sentences or so sufficed in this case. "As I remember it, Miss Hall, you are to retire in five years and want to revise and improve your investment program for retirement. Is that right?"

"Yes. And I want a good investment for my money."

"Of course. Now, you will soon have money available for a rounded investment plan. But meanwhile, you want to get started now on a program that will not tie up all your capital."

"That's exactly right."

With this reconfirmation, the prospect was back on tne beam.

3. Keep It Constructive

I can't emphasize too much the absolute necessity to be constructive. You have told the prospect that you needed time to prepare for this second interview. To close the sale successfully, you've got to show some positive results of your work on his behalf.

(Here you might profitably review Chapter 4. "How To Prepare A Constructive Call.")

Tie Each Point to His Problem—and Wrap It Up

When you *tie* each point in your proposal to the prospect's needs; when he *understands* what it's designed to do; and when he *agrees* it will do it— you're well on your way to the sale. *But you can't take understanding and acceptance for granted just because he's nodding his head.*

You've got to reach for it actively. How?

Mostly by asking: slanting each question directly at the point at issue. Sometimes you can reach for a simple "yes" or "no" answer:

"Do you see how this program guarantees your son's tuition regardless of price changes?" "Do you see how this method helps keep your inventory at just the right level for maintaining a constant flow of production?"

Sometimes you want to avoid a "Yes" or "No" answer. For if you fall into a set pattern, the prospect may start "yessing" you automatically, even when he doesn't understand a point. So mix the questions up.

"How do you think this feature will affect you if inflation continues?" "Does this Settlement Option seem to be the one that best fits into your plans?"

When acceptance is confirmed, move on to the next point. When answers reveal lack of understanding or agreement, repeat the point in different words—then reach for agreement again.

Coding a Presentation

An old friend of mine makes many large and successful intangibles sales by pegging his presentation to a careful analysis of a corporate accounting system. He has a practice other salesmen have adapted to their needs. Let him tell you about it in his own words:

"Most of my sales," says Ralph Burton, "depend on extensive charts showing how my company's system can increase my prospect's accounting efficiency. These charts will differ, of course, in accordance with the prospect's circumstances.

"But in each case I have a little secret code that helps me remember at what point I should stop to make certain everyone present understands the points I am making.

"This code is nothing more than a matter of dots, dashes and exclamation points usually hidden from my prospect by distance. In any case, only *I* know what these little symbols mean: stop and ask a question. That way I'm never too far ahead of my prospect's understanding."

Dramatize It

Burton's story illustrates another point, as well. For his charts demonstrate that he has really done his homework for his prospect—precisely as promised when arranging the second interview.

Any visual device prepared for the occasion will serve the purpose. And by dramatizing your presentation, the visual will strengthen the impact of your story.

How you can use sales tools to best advantage will be detailed in full in Chapter 12. Only two things need be emphasized here.

1. Keep it constructive. Unless the visual stays on the problem-solving track it *doesn't* belong to the second interview procedure.

2. Wrap it up. Unless you stop frequently to ask if he understands and accepts the various points you are making, you'll soon lose your prospect—and your sale.

4. Ask For the Order

You've kept the door open; you've planned your pitch; you've nudged your prospect smack up against the dotted line.

Job finished? Not by a long shot. To earn your keep as a salesman you've still got to ask for the order.

Turn back to Chapter 8 for tips on how to do it best. But do it! Above all, don't be afraid to ask for the order. Remember that the word "no," no matter how forcefully used, is not a brickbat or a gun that can hurt or destroy you!

IN A NUTSHELL

Whether your service requires a two-interview system or whether you're out for a second try because you failed to close the first, you can improve your ratio of sales to second calls by adhering to established guidelines.

First, *sell yourself* into the second interview. Each of the steps you must take becomes a solid stone in your closing foundation.

1. Explain why you will be back– and do it constructively.
2. Close the sale: ask for a *specific* appointment.
3. Follow through.

Second, *plan* your second interview procedures.

1. Remind him why you're there—briefly.
2. Repeat and reconfirm every basic agreement.
3. Keep it constructive.
4. Ask for the order.

10

How to Follow Through
to Repeat Sales

For some, a successful close marks the end of a well-planned presentation. Others see it as the beginning of the next one.

For the top producer, the man who never stops working for one more piece of business, the close is neither end nor beginning. Tempered by persistent follow through, it becomes part of a continuing process, a link in a chain that binds salesman and client together in a mutually profitable relationship. And in this process, the operative phrase is *follow through*.

The president of a major consulting organization spells it out unequivocally. "For too long," he writes, "we have equated salesmanship with the ability to sell the right man the right goods at the right time. Salesmanship does begin with that. But the effective salesman must have the judgment to follow up the sale in a way that insures satisfactory results and increasing business."

Sewing up the initial order is one thing. Sewing up the next order and the one after that takes sophisticated follow through. What follow through can mean in terms of volume and earnings and how you can best apply it will become clear as we explore two broad areas of discussion.

1. Keeping your sale sold.
2. Tested follow through procedures.

I. KEEPING YOUR SALE SOLD

You've sold your man, transformed him from prospect to customer. Keep in touch with him now: see to it that he uses your service to his own best interests—and he will become that most profitable of creatures, a repeat customer. In our competitive era, your score on such conversions ultimately determines your worth as a salesman.

Follow through can insure your sale, protect you from competitive in-roads, pave the way to replacement or adjustment sales. It can open the door to tie-in sales, help you sell more items in your line per customer. And finally, it maximizes radiation, helps you draw more prospects and customers into your selling orbit.

A. INSURE YOUR SALE

Since repeat sales are the backbone of sound business building, no sales-man can afford to ignore one brutal truism: *Your customer is your competitor's prospect.*

Customer Insurance

"Why do you sometimes change suppliers?"

When a group of purchasing agents came to grips with that theme at a recent panel discussion, they wasted little time arriving at some nearly unanimous conclusions. One of the main reasons for making a change, they agreed, was that "a supplier begins to take you for granted." He no longer follows through as once he did when he was hungry for business.

And there's always another salesman who has been trying hard to get your business over a long period of time. He's been giving you the kind of attention you want. So you shift your business to him.

20 Years Down the Drain

In one case, I was called in to find out why a major customer had sud-denly dropped my client after more than 20 years of continual business. "Tom," I asked, during a luncheon meeting with the salesman who serviced that account, "why do you suppose you lost the business?"

"My competitor promised a lot of service he'll never make good on."

"Don't you think he'll try very hard to come through on those promises?"

"Maybe he'll try—but he won't be able to do it."

"As I understand it you normally got your order every June for their annual needs. Is that right?"

"Yes. We had a date for around June 1 every single year for over 20 years. But when I went there this year the business had already been given to this other fellow."

"Did you do anything in a business way to make him aware of your interest in him from one year to the next?"

"Not for several years," Tom admitted. "I did see him at the club practically every week and we'd chat. I really didn't think it was necessary to make any formal calls beyond that."

There's where Tom opened the door to his competitor, as a talk with the customer revealed. Sometimes, for example, shipments had not arrived on time. While complaints had been made to management, Tom had not followed up to see that it didn't happen again. Nor had he known that at times the competing salesman had been on hand with the answer when some servicing problems came up.

"Customer Insurance:" Planned Follow Through

Taking the customer for granted may be a sure fire way of losing a long standing account. But many a salesman forfeits repeat sales possibilities from the very beginning.

Unlike the route man who attends to his customer's wants on a daily or weekly schedule, the intangibles salesman does not normally do business with his customers on a regular basis. Rather, he makes occasional calls to his clients as particular situations arise that require his services.

Because he does not bend his schedule to recurring rhythms, the intangibles salesman can easily neglect follow through procedures. You can best avoid this fatal oversight by planning for follow up activities as part of your regular schedule.

George Tisdale learned this the hard way. George sells mainly to professionals and businessmen who use the information services of the publishing house he represents to keep up to date on various aspects of their operations.

A large percentage of George's earnings comes from renewals which to some degree are automatic. Furthermore, his company actively cultivates renewal business by direct mail. Of course, regardless of how these renewals originate, George collects his commissions.

Looking at this situation from the outside, you would conclude that George really had it made. Yet for a long time he struggled to keep himself going.

"One day," he says, "I realized I had to pull down more repeat sales— or quit selling. After a lot of thought I saw that the trouble was of my own making. Because I could count on our direct mail campaigns for some renewals, I had completely neglected *personal* follow through.

"I'd make a sale, then forget it while I went after another prospect. Now I decided on a big rebuilding job with my former customers. After all, I had done a good educational job on them in the first place—so why lose the benefit of this to some other salesman?

"Nor did I want to neglect my present prospects. Working that out led me to study my business in a way I had never done before. I found that 60% of my commissions came from sales to attorneys, 20% from sales to accountants, and another 20% from sales to businesses. When I checked these figures out with my boss, he told me they were almost exactly in line with our other men.

"The rest was easy. First I figured out how much time to allow for follow up. Then I divided that time proportionately on the same 60–20–20 basis.

"Sure, I can still count on those automatic renewals. But the bulk of my repeat business comes in because my customers can now count on me to check out their needs."

Adjustments Count, Too

In many intangibles fields the salesman may have no renewal or replacement sales to look forward to. But given the same kind of planned and persistent follow through he can make room for *adjustment* sales.

The man who buys term insurance today may be able to afford regular life tomorrow, and might add a policy on his wife for good measure. Yesterday's $200-a-month investor may escalate to a $500-a-month investment plan when his big promotion comes through.

And that's the broader lesson concealed in the George Tisdale story. For such adjustment sales do *not* happen of themselves—anymore than George's renewals do. You must set the stage for them with your own follow through.

B. "SELL MATES" AND TIE-INS

When you capitalize on the sale of one item in your line to sell a natural companion piece, you've made a tie-in sale. The most familiar "sell mates" are the tie that matches the shirt, the socks that go with the shoes, the gloves that set off the handbag.

Study Your Combinations

Intangibles tie-ins may not be so obvious. But for the man who studies the natural "sell mates" combinations in his own business, they represent a real opportunity.

The speculative investor might like to balance his portfolio with a dependable income producer—and vice versa. The mutual funds buyer might find it useful to have leverage funds—if you follow up with that "sell mates" suggestion.

Prudential has signaled the trend toward broadened insurance lines. The Prudential agent must soon be a total insurance man who can use one sale as a springboard for selling other items in the line. The householder who insures his possessions against fire can surely be led to protect them against theft. Follow through on automobile insurance can suggest the need for hospitalization coverage.

Whatever your field, successful cross-selling begins with a search for such natural "sell mates." List *all* the services in your line, then match up the combinations.

Post-Sale Inquiry

As with renewals and replacement sales, so with tie-ins: they will *not* happen of their own accord. You've got to aim for it consciously, go after it actively.

Many banks, for example, sell more than 150 services: most of them with excellent "sell mates" potential. Yet studies disclose that the average customer buys only two to four of those services—though he could use 25–30 of them for business or personal needs.

But those few banks which have pushed cross selling and offered training in follow through inquiry have registered a tremendous advance over their competitors in the ratio of services sold per customer. Where pre-sale inquiry spotlights customer problems, post-sale inquiry pinpoints the tie-in possibilities.

One officer tells of a sale which he freely admits would have been lost in the shuffle before the bank's new tie-in orientation. This banker returned from lunch just as a teller was completing a traveler's check transaction.

"Not bad being an importer," the teller remarked. "You get to see the world."

Pointing to the customer who was heading for the door, he added: "Mr. Wilde is off to South America this time."

"Because our training sessions had made me highly sell conscious," says the officer, "this gave me an idea. After giving the customer a chance to get back to his office, I phoned. 'Mr. Wilde,' I said, 'I understand you're making a business trip to South America.'

'That's right. I may be away for three months.'

'Do you ever have occasion to make security transactions when you're traveling?'

'I often do.'

'Does your wife take care of them at such times?'

'That's right.'

'Would you find it convenient if our bank handled such transactions for you: relieving you and your wife of the bother and worry?"

'I never thought of that,' the customer exclaimed."

Because of this follow through inquiry he not only thought of it—he arranged for it, too.

Leave the Door Open

Given the nature of intangibles sales, you can't always push for an immediate tie-in, let alone jump in with some unrelated item. But you can pave the way for a follow up sale at a later date.

Here's how David Bates does it. "Mr. Kingsley, I believe you will find that these municipal bonds will give you the kind of security you were looking for. However, I do feel you will want to balance your portfolio soon with growth holdings. Is that right?"

"Well, it does sound right."

"Then if some very special offering comes up that you may not have been able to learn about elsewhere, may I call you and tell you about it?"

"I'd appreciate it."

Having completed a rather sizable transaction, Dave backs away from any immediate attempt to close a tie-in sale. But he leaves a very powerful thought with the prospect that will fertilize the soil, so to speak, for a subsequent follow up call.

In this case, a good securities salesman will recognize the need to keep records of customers' holdings so that he can be on hand with plans for the investment of funds when bonds mature or are called. Many's the sale lost by otherwise good salesmen of securities who don't pay attention to such details.

C. RADIATION

There is one very obvious, very lucrative—but often overlooked—follow through query you can make right after you close the sale.

"Mr. Rose, you have seen how this plan will help meet your specific needs. I wonder if you know anyone else with similar needs and problems who could be helped in the same way?"

This simple follow up has meant millions of dollars in sales to those who use it. It can mean many extra dollars to you and your firm if you apply it habitually.

Like so many of the techniques which work for the best salesman, this is one which average men either forget or fear to use. Some of us who do believe in and use this technique and others know that they work, and use them as a matter of practice. I have seldom found a client unwilling to help me get more business, though some may give me a name and ask that I not use theirs in my approach—a request I always respect. Others have gone so far as to provide introductions and even make calls and appointments for me.

Service Plus

After you have closed a sale, delivered it properly, and serviced it well, you should begin to get a broader range of prospects. A truly satisfied customer will often lead to the best kind of radiation—prospects he brings in on his own.

Henry Geyer sells a maintenance plan to homeowners. This is an intensely competitive business: if you don't keep an eye on the servicing problem you can kiss your customer goodbye.

"I get a lot of good leads from my customers," he says, "because I give them good service *plus*."

"What do you mean, 'service plus?' " I asked.

"Every firm in our field gives pretty good service. But I add a plus. I call the customer the day after our men have serviced him, just to ask if everything is all right."

"What makes this extra call so important?"

"Sometimes I catch things that weren't handled right. But there's more to it than that. These 'plus' calls show the customers that I'll go out of my way to help them.

"And it's a pretty good bet that they'll talk about the kind of attention they get from me when someone kicks about the poor service he's getting from another maintenance outfit. Or if I have a prospect he knows, I can usually get one of my customers to call him and tell him about the follow up service I do for them."

2. TESTED FOLLOW THROUGH PROCEDURES

What the buyer thinks and how he feels after placing an order will determine if he will buy again. And how you follow up the order will determine what he thinks.

Not that it takes much to cement his good will. If you're appreciative; if you can be depended upon for proper delivery; if you're available for servicing when required—you'll keep the sale sold.

Sure, most every salesman tries to demonstrate gratitude, dependability and willingness to render personal service. But in each of these areas I'm talking about that all important *extra* step, the step that gives you a competitive edge.

A. BE APPRECIATIVE

One of the basic rules of selling is to acknowledge orders—with thanks.

Large order or small, tell the buyer you are glad to have his business. And never fail to say "thank you" by mail, phone or in person. Not to do so is one of the common reasons for failure to get repeat business.

Gratitude Plus

Above we mentioned the importance of the extra step. For where everyone says "thanks" it takes an added touch to make your gesture of appreciation stand out. One simple way is to offer follow through service with your thanks.

One salesman does this religiously via a post card follow up. "I make it a point to send out a 'thank you' note acknowledging every order *and inviting the customer to get in touch with me if he needs my help.* I find I can do this with the least time and trouble by sending out post cards in the evening after the day's work."

Another salesman, who also emphasizes his eagerness to serve the client, underscores the point by enclosing a choice selection of helpful brochures with his "thank you" note.

Thank Him for Helping You

One point connected with the vital "thank you" gesture tends to be overlooked. That is, to let the client know how much you gained from your association with him, how working with him has helped you get new business—and how much you appreciate all this.

Needless to say, this must be real and sincere. When it is, your gesture can almost guarantee future business when the need arises.

B. BE DEPENDABLE

A reputation for extra care and dependability in follow through can be a tremendous asset to any salesman. When the customer can always count on you to come through on every promise (or conversely, to promise only what you know you can deliver), then your personal relations are built on solid bedrock.

Dependability must be demonstrated more in the *doing* than in the telling. This means four things in particular:

● Make constructive delivery.
● Keep on top of the sale.
● Make sure they're happy.
● Keep them informed.

1. Constructive Delivery

The secret of successful delivery lies in being constructive, in demonstrating that your interest in the client does not end with the order. You can review what he bought, bring in a "plus," offer to be of service.

REVIEW WHAT HE BOUGHT

I have seen salesmen march into a man's office, slap an insurance policy on his desk and say, "There's your policy; I hope you like it. You'd better put it in a safe deposit box."

And out they go—neither offering another word nor waiting for one in reply. Perhaps they feel that the sight of the policy is enough to make the customer swoon with delight and wait eagerly for another chance to buy.

Actually, however important the sale is to you, it represents only one small element in the life of your client. He may have completely forgotten the matter or nearly so, given the pressure of other affairs. That's why he'll appreciate it if you run through the high spots again—if you tell him briefly what he bought and what it will do for him.

Maybe you went over it many times before making the sale. But to keep him sold, review the key points one last time when you make delivery.

It pays.

DELIVERY PLUS

The extra step in delivery can take a variety of forms. Reviewing what the customer bought is actually one of them. Bringing in a tangible plus is another.

Robert Ackerman sells a maintenance service to manufacturers who need reliable lubricants. He has built a respectable income by consistently bringing along something extra when he checks delivery.

"For example, after I made my first small sale to a builder of diesel engines, I brought in a detailed chart showing how lubricants could be specified for each type of engine they manufacture. They had us in mind only as a back-up supplier originally, but my chart gave them the idea of printing that information for their complete line in booklets they give to their customers.

"As a result, we now supply nearly all of their lubricating needs, and get quite a few of their customers to boot."

OFFER TO BE OF SERVICE

This speaks for itself—and there'll be more on service later. The main thing is to stress your desire to be of service when you make or check out delivery.

2. Keep On Top Of the Sale

Some salesmen make a special point of following the first business they receive from a new customer from the very beginning right through completion. Or if need be, they can tell him exactly what went wrong and what can be done about it.

Good as this is, it isn't enough. For as we have seen, old customers can cut you out once you let down on follow up procedures.

One crack freight forwarding salesman has snagged the lion's share from many a competitor by the simple expedient of giving his customer personal attention *on each major shipment*. Let him tell how he does this in a typical case.

"My repeat sales with one large furniture manufacturer begin when I check the pick-up with the traffic manager. First I find out what he did or did not like about the way we handled the equipment.

"If he's happy about it, I tell him we'll do all we can to maintain the quality of our service. If he's not, I assure him we'll correct matters now and take steps to improve our service in the future.

"Three years ago we sold this account only rarely. By following this pattern, I have been able to increase our sales to the point where we are now the major forwarder."

Here we see the reverse side of a coin we flipped before. Earlier I pointed out that your customer is your competitor's prospect. Equally, *his customers are your prospects*. But more on this below.

3. Make Sure They're Happy

Many repeat sales are lost *after* the sale is made—even though the buyer is fully satisfied with what he bought.

Why?

Only because the salesman loses interest in the product or service he just sold. Many a buyer has echoed this typical complaint voiced in a letter to *Sales Management*. "I never hear from the salesman after I buy—until he wants his next order.

"He never *asks* if I'm getting proper use from his product or service after delivery. He never *checks* on whether adjustments are necessary, never *looks in* to see if I have any questions in mind. *I don't like to buy from such salesmen again,* unless I must."

INQUIRE FOR POST-SALE INSURANCE

In contrast to the above, one man has built up a solid backlog of repeat business by consistent post-sale inquiry. This follow through begins with the detailed notations he makes at the point of sale. Then after several weeks he follows up the outcome of the order.

"Is the service operating as smoothly as I said it would?" he wants to know. "Has the desired application worked out as promised?"

Then he presses on with more specific questions. "Has our service cut down on labor costs in general? Has it reduced overtime expenditure?" And so on.

Where the answer is "no," he comes around to see why and to make any indicated adjustments. Sure, this takes time—but much of it is done on his regular rounds or by telephone. More to the point, this dependable follow through pays off in increasingly high earnings. For in effect it serves as the preliminary investigation for the next sale.

And it can be done so simply. Salesmen who sell airline services will call a new customer after he has returned from a trip. Was the service satisfactory? Does he have any complaints that might be taken care of next time?

This simple follow through will often spell the difference between landing the "next time" sale or losing it to a competitor.

Frequently when I have mentioned this idea to an individual or to groups of salesmen, they protest that it's "dangerous"—that if something had gone wrong they might lose the business. My contention is that there is *less* danger of losing the business, even if something did go wrong, than there will be if you simply neglect to enquire.

In my own business all of us working together make it a consistent practice to see if what we have done for the client measures up to his expectations. Sometimes, of course, we get a negative response, but at least we have a chance either to amend the work—or to justify what has seemed like poor performance to him.

My sincere advice is: Don't be afraid to ask.

4. Keep Them Informed

As in many areas of life, just doing the job may not be enough. Sometimes you've got to toot your own horn: let people know what you're doing.

Any good advertising agency account executive, as but one example, spends a substantial part of his time keeping his clients posted on what the agency is doing, why they are doing it, and what results they have achieved. One man has been doing this on a monthly basis for one of his major clients.

"Ever since I got this account," he says, "I have made it a point to file monthly reports with the principal officers of the company. These reports cover every aspect of the job we're doing for them. This sort of reporting has helped us keep that account for more years than other firms, including our own, have done with most clients."

"I HAVE NEVER YET LOST A CUSTOMER"

This practice could be followed more often, and with profit, in less glamorous businesses. Of course, one should do it sparingly. And the effect should be one of offering another follow up service, rather than of personal puffery.

Some years ago, I became acquainted with Denton Johnson of the freight division of a major airline. "Abbott," he told me one day, "I have never yet lost a customer I've personally sold."

"That's an extraordinary accomplishment for any salesman," I exclaimed. "How do you account for it?"

"It's really very simple. When I get business from a company, I always get a report on the packaging of the items shipped, on the labeling, on the delivery of the item to us or on our own pick up service.

"When we make the delivery, I ask for a report on the date and on the condition of the merchandise when received. And I verify this with the receiver.

"Once I have all these reports, I take them to my client and tell him exactly how we handled his shipment. I back this up with the report forms which in themselves demonstrate how much interest I take in his business.

"In addition, I try to come up with helpful suggestions based on these reports. In most cases I can, showing how he can cut down on weight, speed the handling of his shipment, or whatever. Invariably, this results in more —and often bigger—shipments."

The last paragraph illustrates reporting *plus*—the extra touch that stands out when when keeping your principals posted.

Follow Through on Turndowns

The successful salesman doesn't stop with following through on sales. He follows up unproductive calls with a letter or phone call to acknowledge the courtesy shown in the interview—and to inform the prospect that he's still hopeful of serving him in the future. From time to time, he keeps the contact alive with other calls.

For the buyer who brushes you off today may suddenly come to need your service tomorrow. By expressing appreciation and by keeping in touch, the future-minded salesman often gets favorable attention when the buyer is finally ready to buy.

Turndowns Turn Him On

Few general insurance men can approach Clair Devlin in volume or earnings. Living in an area with a high percentage of frame dwellings, Clair does an outstanding job on fire insurance: putting himself well ahead of his closest competitors. As he tells it:

"I come pretty near to selling 75% of all the people in this town and the surrounding area some fire insurance. Sure, other agencies get a good share of this business too—but I tack on the extra insurance that makes the difference in many cases between adequate and inadequate coverage.

"My secret? It's mostly a matter of organized follow through on turndowns. I engage a clipping bureau that sends me fire disaster stories from every newspaper in this state. When someone says he won't do business with me because he's insured by another agency, I start a follow-up campaign built around those clippings."

Clair mails these stories out in envelopes distinctively marked with a flame symbol in the upper left hand corner. Attached to the clipping is a card with his name on it. The message reads: "This could happen to you: for *complete* protection call Claire Devlin to analyze your coverage."

"After sending three or four of these clippings to the person who turned me down," says Clair, "I telephone the prospect. A surprisingly large number will now let me check on whether or not they have sufficient insurance on their dwellings and contents."

Do It On a Smaller Scale

Not that your turndown follow throughs need be so elaborate. Elmer Reisman, who represents a well-established lighting contractor, converts many a turndown into a lucrative contract simply by keeping in touch via occasional phone calls.

Even when he makes no sale, Elmer sends a follow up letter expressing thanks for the interview, touching briefly on the main points the prospect had accepted, and telling him he will be glad to review the situation again should the prospect have any second thoughts about his lighting needs.

From that point on, he telephones the prospect occasionally. Sometimes he'll offer a new idea for modernizing or improving the prospect's lighting system. At other times he'll simply ask if the existing layout still does the job adequately. In the end, this persistence pays off in a sufficient number of cases to keep Elmer in the earning bracket he requires.

He Follows Through on His Competitors' Sales

Here is an outstanding application of follow through by a man who obviously never stops trying. The same freight forwarding salesman referred to above, he makes a reality of my earlier statement: "Your competitor's customers are your prospects."

"From my own experience," this man says, "I know that even my own firm can't always come through on an order as promised. Thus I have found that a post-order follow through on my competitor's sale will often pay dividends. For it puts me in a position to take up the slack.

"When a competitor beats me out, I'll call the customer back on the day of the scheduled pick up. Only two days ago, for example, the competing firm couldn't get through because of a last minute breakdown. One of our trucks happened to be in the vicinity and I was able to arrange for an immediate pick up.

"When everything is in order, I ask if the pick up and delivery were satisfactory. Either way, the customer appreciates this follow up and keeps me in mind for future business."

There is what I call a rampant myth that one should not "knock competitors" or look for weaknesses in their services. This seems to some people a kind of high pressure behavior that they find distasteful. In my experience it has not worked out that way. Many of my customers over the years have become customers and friends because I was able to find the weaknesses of my competitors, and then to point out my company's strengths. I do *not* mean fault finding or pointless criticism, but instead, using knowledge of competitive weakness which could be harmful to your client.

It would be foolish to concentrate too much of one's energy on this kind of activity, or to depend on it for sales. Nevertheless, a certain awareness of the opportunities that lie in keeping yourself alert to failures and weaknesses in competitive services is just plain good business and good selling. Champion athletes often win this way, and so can you in the game of salesmanship.

When Your Competitor Cuts Corners

Sometimes a competitor will win out because of a quote based on a sacrifice of quality. Often you won't know this is so until it's too late. But if you sense something in the wind you can investigate and follow up with another call before the contract is signed.

In such cases, however, knocking the competition directly may negate the effect of your discoveries. Just alert the prospect with a pointed follow-through query and let him draw his own conclusions.

A salesman for a firm that designs industrial cooling systems tells of one such instance when a contractor asked for quotes on the design and equipment for a walk-in meat cooler. Underbid by a competitor, Sandy Lockman was sure something was lacking in the low-priced quote. After checking into the matter with his own management, Sandy was ready to reopen the case a week later.

First he alerted the prospect by asking: "Has your other bidder quoted on a tower and circulation pump to prevent wasting water?"

The contractor looked up the specifications. There was no such provision.

Now Sandy pressed his advantage by asking: "Will your customer stand for water bills he'll get with the installation wasting 1,800 gallons per hour?"

This follow up of a competitor's bid retrieved an apparently lost sale.

The lesson is clear. To prove dependability, follow through in some way on every interview, successful or not.

C. BE AVAILABLE

In many intangibles fields, service means simply being available. It means keeping in touch with your client to see that he's using the service to his best advantage; it means being on tap to answer his queries; it means checking out his situation from time to time to see if adjustments are indicated.

Most intangibles salesmen know their services will do the job once delivered or installed. But the buyer only *hopes* this will be so. He likes to feel the salesman will be around to do something about it should anything go wrong.

1. Coordinated Service Contacts

In many intangibles fields the buyer neither expects nor receives personal attention after he makes his purchase. So, for example, the policy holder who sends his premiums in by mail. The trouble is, the salesman fails to reap the full benefit from such sales because he can hardly build up repeat business with little or no servicing contacts.

Some salesmen avoid this blind-alley situation by planning coordinated campaigns which minimize in-person follow ups. For example, Ray Bayles' post-sale campaign starts with the delivery of the policy in person.

After that, he makes personal visits very infrequently. But he phones fairly often to see if the customer has any question in mind. At the same time he probes deeply enough to judge if the customer is ripe for increased coverage or for some other insurance service. And every quarter he canvasses his clients with a mailing that describes whatever plan the recipient may respond to.

Ray launched this follow through plan five years ago. By bringing in more volume per customer, it has enabled him to ease his work load, have more time for his family, and still enjoy a modest increase in earnings.

2. Service Plus

A coordinated follow up campaign such as the one described may be a sufficient plus in personal sales. But in a competitive high volume business—especially where you handle a broad line of services—repeat sales may hang on a more imaginative extra.

For example, when the potential value warrants the time and effort expended, Wilfred Cooper makes regular spot-checks on the way his service is working on a once-a-week or once-a-month basis, according to need. Naturally, he lets the customer know what he's doing. And he assures him that when something important comes up, he will bring it to his attention immediately.

"You would be surprised," says Wilfred, "how many people have told me of this procedure of mine in the course of casual conversation with other manufacturers. To my own knowledge, I have received many pieces of new business simply because of this plan. And it is the one biggest reason I have been able to hold on to our old accounts with few losses over the years to competitors."

Here we see how being available promotes radiation as well as repeat business.

SERVICE IN DEPTH

If in some intangibles fields personal availability is a luxury, in others it is a necessity. A plus in such cases will pay off big.

Not long ago I discussed the servicing factor with Rudy Casals, who deals in office systems. "In my business," Rudy told me, "a sale is never completed. I keep in touch with my customers for a long, long time after they make a purchase. I don't bother them with social calls, but I do go around frequently to be sure things are working out well. Personally, I consider this as much a part of my job as getting the order."

"What do you do specifically on these follow up calls?" I asked.

"An office systems purchase inevitably requires serious changes in the practices and procedures of the buying company. Many of the people who must do the actual work can get all fouled up for a while. I try to make it easy for them by making myself available to help even the lowest level of personnel.

"This means going way down the line—talking with clerks, bookkeepers, secretaries and other operating personnel. Word of this kind of help sooner or later gets back up top and puts me in line for future business.

"Only the other day, an important customer called me up after hearing about the pains I took with some of his lower level employees. 'Rudy,' he told me, 'it's great to know a salesman who doesn't disappear as soon as he makes the sale.'"

You don't have to worry about losing a client who feels that way about your servicing efforts.

3. Be Available for Questions

Be on tap to smooth over exchanges, speed in a spare part; arrange for a fast repair job or the like and you'll probably rate high on availability for the buyer of tangible products. To some extent, the same holds true with intangibles; but there the high scorer must reckon with another dimension as well.

For at intervals, a question or two may nag at the intangibles customer as he contemplates your plan. And he likes to count on your availability with the answers when he wants them.

THEY'RE AS CLOSE TO YOU AS YOUR PHONE

Here is where the intangibles salesman finds telephone follow ups especially useful. Expending a minimum of time, he gains a maximum of coverage.

To this end, Karl Bach, of Penn Mutual Life Insurance in San Francisco, employs a unique follow through device of his own designing. Upon completing a sale, he invites his customers to call him collect whenever they have any problems or questions requiring immediate attention.

In his book, *How I Sell $12,000,000 of Life Insurance Year After Year,* he cites one of many cases where this policy paid off handsomely.

The story opens with a young man buying a modest life insurance policy from Bach just before being called up as a naval officer. After thanking him for his business, Bach invited the customer to phone collect from wherever he might be whenever he had questions about the policy in particular or insurance in general.

From time to time this young man and his wife phoned Bach from various parts of the country to pose one or another query. Always Bach patiently passed along the requested information.

One day, Bach received a collect call from New York. After a brief chat, the wife came on. "Karl," she said, "my husband just got a big promotion. We want a $100,000 policy on him and a $10,000 policy each on me and the children."

That, you will agree, was a fine bonus for the willingness to listen—and pay for it!

4. The Periodic Review

Of course, you will recognize this story as part of the how-to of gaining an adjustment sale—the "repeat" sale of the intangibles salesman who keeps in touch with his customer's changing circumstances.

Yet Bach's method, however successful, may seem a little bit too essentially passive for some of us. For it relies on the customer's initiative to bring it off.

A more positive way is to arrange for a periodic review of the customer's situation. Such a periodic check of the client's personal or business circumstances can be one of the most constructive—and productive—follow through procedures. Securities salesman Peter Morrison can testify to that.

Most of his customers agree that regularly scheduled review of their portfolios and personal needs makes sense. Pete tells what happened in a recent case which began with a somewhat modest investment.

"But my very first review appointment came on the heels of a substantial raise in pay for my customer. Now he was interested in working out a plan for building up his estate. With careful questioning, I got important details about his job situation, his family and some real estate properties he owned. We agreed to meet again the following week."

Together with his department manager, Pete analyzed the client's assets and checked over his portfolio. The estate as it then stood, they agreed, was highly vulnerable to taxes. It was clear, too, that the customer's investments should be more diversified. And so Pete came to the appointed meeting with some initial recommendations for remedying those conditions.

His client went along with the plan. They have now had several review conferences. In every case but one this has led to broadened sales.

Perhaps it's a matter of temperament. Some, like Karl Bach, may prefer to make it easy for the client to come to them. Others, like Peter Morrison, prefer to keep the initiative in their own hands.

However you do it, keeping on top of the client's situation is good for him and good business for you.

REVIEWING YOUR INDUSTRY SITUATION

If anything, Jerry Cardell is even higher on the potentialities of the periodic review than Peter Morrison.

"Maybe I'm kidding myself," Jerry once told me, "but I think there's an unlimited potential in such reviews for any intangibles salesman. And the beauty of it is that you needn't confine yourself to changes in the *customer's* circumstances. You can also take advantage of changes in your own business."

"What exactly do you mean by that?" I inquired.

"Well, take my own field. The insurance business has developed single policies which now cover more risks than before. For instance, you can buy policies now which in one contract cover almost all the needs of a homeowner. And the big buyer of business protection can now buy single contracts for coverage which formerly required several.

"This means the buyer has only one premium to pay when he gives all his business to one agent. And he has only one agency to deal with on claims.

"The man who follows through consistently has the inside track when his periodic review spotlights the gains to be made by taking advantage of business changes. He's the one who chalks up the adjustment sale—and he can often beef up one or more parts of the consolidated contract in the bargain."

CAPSULE SUMMARY

In our competitive era, a salesman has no greater responsibility than to serve present customers in a way that warrants their continuing business. Planned follow through represents built-in "customer insurance"—protecting future sales against competitive inroads.

Repeat sales are only the beginning. As intangibles firms broaden their line of services, new opportunities open up for those who follow through effectively. Study your line for natural "sell mates," let each serve as a bridge connecting one sale to the next, and you will merit respect and more business if you inquire into your clients' other needs frequently; needs which you are in a position to fill.

The key to effective follow through is to go one step further than your competitors might go. When you say "thank you" for the order, let the customer know how anxious you are to serve him well.

Then prove it in the doing.

When you make delivery, review the plan for him. Be sure that every aspect of your sale is understood by everyone involved.

Check again later to make sure your client is happy with your service. Probe deeply enough to be sure no loose ends or rough edges remain.

Ask him specific questions. Ask if he's getting along all right under your program. Ask if he's making progress in every area your service affects. Ask if he needs help in using it to his best advantage.

Finally, keep yourself available for servicing. Stay in touch by phone, by mail or in person. Arrange to be on tap when he has an urgent question in mind. Keep current with his changing situation—perhaps by scheduling periodic reviews.

You'll keep more of your customers longer when you follow through in that manner.

11

How to Put Yourself Out In Front

in Intangibles Selling

"First you've got to sell yourself."

Somewhere along the line you've probably heard a seasoned salesman express the point in exactly those words. For most representatives know that one basic difference between the top producer and the average salesman is that the former has mastered the act of cultivating sound customer relations. And in so doing, he has gained the inside track on the major source of continued and growing income.

Selling yourself is perhaps even more important for the intangibles salesman than for most. His is apt to be a highly personalized form of salesmanship: tied more firmly to the individual salesman than in the selling of tangibles.

For in handling intangibles we very often deal with the intimate problems of an individual or with the "personal problems" of a business. To do a good job we must necessarily immerse ourselves in the confidential affairs of our clients. Before they'll open their secrets to our view, these clients must be sold on us personally.

By the same token, as a salesman you do not jump from one intangibles field to another as readily as do men who sell products. Since your knowledge of existing customers represents a valuable asset, you will hardly toss it aside lightly. Having sold yourself early in the game, you will want to keep on reaping the benefits of the personal customer good will you have built up.

The Fruits of Good Will

A tremendous amount of business turns essentially upon such personal relationships, especially where the programs and prices of competing firms are essentially the same. Indeed, in some cases competitors have actually offered greater benefits or lower prices—only to see the order go to the salesman who has sold himself to best advantage. And in other cases buyers probably more often than not, award business to salesmen who have sold themselves effectively, without even waiting for a competitive offer.

Sure, you may know all this. But it's a good bet that you have never been trained to sell yourself in an organized manner. Like most salesmen you have undoubtedly built closer relationships by picking up the tab for lunch or drinks, buying tickets for a show, talking about matters closest to the client's heart, and the like.

While such things do play a part, selling yourself goes much deeper than the personal touch alone. For the most part, you can build or improve upon your customer relationships—making them more *profitable* as well as more *enduring*—by focusing on the following areas:

- Build on a firm foundation.
- Win the customer's confidence.
- Help them keep you in mind.
- Cultivate new contacts.

A. BUILD ON A FIRM FOUNDATION

Selling yourself has sometimes been treated, rather misleadingly, in terms of personality. Thus we get the popular picture of the super-salesman "personality kid" whose charm and enthusiasm make all and sundry rush over to sign on the dotted line.

Actually, few successful salesmen can be fitted into any preconceived personality pattern. As Carl Hoffman, partner in a major consulting firm, has said: "We must throw out the notion that the good salesman conforms to some ideal 'personality profile.' *Anyone can sell himself and his services if he treats the customer as a man with a problem to be solved*—not as someone to be manipulated into a sale."

Hoffman's words strikingly echo the theme of Chapter 4. For there we saw that the *constructive call*—designed precisely to help the "man with a problem to be solved"—puts you into the most favored position for your selling interview. It beats out personality; it beats out price; and on occasion, it beats out friendship, too.

The Buyer's Best Friend

Not that friendship will hurt—especially for intangibles geared to the personal level. For one thing, however, you won't normally build consistent volume on friendship alone. For another, the word takes on a different meaning during business hours.

As the Director of Purchasing of Allied Chemicals sums it up: "The salesman who calls with some useful ideas in his head is the buyer's best friend."

A pleasant smile, coupled to a genuine interest in people, will inspire friendly relationships. But they'll go much deeper from a selling standpoint when they rest upon a solid foundation of constructive habits.

An Idea Triples Sales Volume

Once you start thinking in terms of ideas, selling yourself becomes infinitely more exciting. For it opens up a whole new world of selling opportunities.

True, it also takes a lot of work. You must constantly pile up information on the customer's business, read trade publications, ask questions. But given the complex and competitive nature of marketing today, selling yourself with ideas can be one of the most rewarding avenues to increased earnings.

Several years ago, Anton Dichter, whose service equipment is used for industrial purposes, took over an account from a fellow salesman who was moving out to the West Coast. This man explained that he supplied about 30% of the customer's requirements only because he and the buyer were personal friends. Let Anton tell the rest of the story.

"I figured if that was as far as he could go on a friendship, I'd better have something more meaningful going for me. After all, I had never yet met the buyer.

"Before making my first call, I looked into the situation pretty carefully. The plant was in a town about 60 miles from our offices so the customer always had trouble getting parts for emergency jobs—from us and from his other suppliers. There was always a phone call, plus transportation expenses which had to be added to the bill.

"When I came in for my initial order, I first outlined my idea. I suggested installing bins in their supply room, and labeling them by part name and number of parts to be kept on hand. On every subsequent call I would inventory those parts and file replacement orders if necessary. The emergency flaps, the extra time and the extra expenditures all evaporated.

"Ever since that time, I make it a point to bring in a new idea on every other call at least. One time it might do with applications, another time with maintenance.

"Practically overnight, I gained a friendly respect from this buyer. By now, my volume from this account is three times as great as our other salesman had built up on friendship alone."

Ideas are indeed a buyer's best friend . . . and the salesman's, too.

It Doesn't Have To Relate

The ideas Anton brings in when cultivating good relations tend to be connected to the operation of his service. But this need not be the case. Nor, for that matter, does an idea that sells you to the client necessarily have to be the product of long study and effort.

What counts is making a habit of selling yourself by constructive means.

Consider the case of the bank officer who was handed the account of a large laundry which maintained modest balances with this bank. His customer showed a net profit in the previous year of 8%, whereas the average for the industry as shown in the Morris Statement Studies came to less than 3%. Other ratios were equally favorable. Obviously, here was an account which could be nursed to more profitable levels, given careful cultivation.

As it happens, the bank had recently installed a sales training program for its contact officers. Since that program had also stressed the importance of constructive calls in building good relations, this officer was wondering, more or less idly, where he could find a good idea for his next call in which he planned to suggest a line of credit.

On his previous contact, the officer discovered that his client had recently opened a coin laundry across town from its home office and plant. If successful, it was to be the forerunner of a chain of automatic laundries —which would surely open up interesting financing possibilities.

Several days before his appointment at the home office, the banker dropped in at the coin laundry. A discussion with the attendant disclosed that business was on the slow side, even though no laundries of any kind were available in the general neighborhood. And, he noted, there was only one dry cleaning outlet in a tailor shop two blocks away.

That gave the officer his idea. When he called, he told his customer frankly that he felt the coin laundry was not doing as well as it might. "Do you think it might help to use the place also as a receiving station for general laundry and dry cleaning which could be done at this plant?"

"Now that's an idea I should have thought of," the owner exclaimed. He picked up the phone, relayed the idea to an assistant and asked him to start working on it.

When he was through, he was in a receptive mood for the officer's proposition. And sure enough, the banker achieved his first major financing breakthrough with a man whose credit needs had mostly been serviced by a competing institution.

For as the customer put it: "I really must give consideration to a banker who thinks as constructively about my business as you do!"

Clearly, the client was sold on the banker personally. But note that the idea related to "my business"—*not* the banker's.

This suggests that any intangibles salesman who had dealings with that customer could have sold himself with the identical idea—had he thought of it first. He might have been selling business insurance; he might have been selling securities.

Whatever he was selling, the road to that man's heart would be a road paved with constructive ideas.

Turn on the charm if you will; flash that smile; toss in a cheery "hello." But if you want a profitable business relationship, sell yourself with ideas.

By-Products and Antidotes

As a by-product—and a valuable one at that—you will find yourself with an antidote to idea staleness.

Many an intangibles salesman must work with an organized presentation —a canned sales talk, if you will. In the beginning, it helps a man take hold. But years of such sameness can dampen anyone's enthusiasm, smother his creativity.

Sooner or later, everything goes flat, even if for only a short time. He may force himself to make the same dreary rounds, but productivity inevitably tails off.

Once you develop the habit of selling yourself constructively, you've got a built-in antidote. With every call pregnant with ideas, you take the curse off an organized presentation. The framework remains; the details constantly change. And the more consistently you pump in fresh material, the longer your story stays alive in your mind.

B. WIN YOUR CUSTOMER'S CONFIDENCE

You can best gain your customer's confidence by demonstrating your sincere concern for his welfare. Taking pains to come in with helpful ideas was your first step in this direction. You can complete the job in two ways, primarily. Be dependable; keep him informed.

BE DEPENDABLE

Here we see a natural overlap with the techniques of follow through. When you make good on your promises of performance and servicing, you have surely sold the client on your dependability.

Don't Oversell

But now we go beyond that. Winning your customer's confidence starts with being realistic about everything you say. Above all, it means promising only what you can deliver.

For if confidence is built slowly, it can be shattered quickly. Let your client once feel that you are solving your problems at his expense, and your personal image can be smashed for good.

Say, for example, you haven't been closing many sales in a given period. The pressure is on for you to produce.

In such circumstances you can easily be tempted to oversell: to talk the unwary customer into a deal he doesn't really need. Then up goes the automatic sales resistance banner on every subsequent call. Maybe you bailed yourself out—but at the cost of future commissions.

I remember a moment I spent with a salesman who was on his way out to an appointment. His boss had told me the man was one of the most consistent big money earners in the securities field.

"I can only give you a couple of minutes," this man said when I approached him.

"Can you tell me what you see as the one most important factor in building up a regular clientele?" I asked.

Without a moment's hesitation he replied: "Don't oversell."

"Can you elaborate on that point in the minute or so you've got left?"

"I have never deliberately oversold. Sometimes I have consciously undersold where a customer inquired about an issue I wasn't sure of. The people I deal with *know* they can count on what I tell them. And I can count on them."

In the course of several interviews, the customer will spot such integrity. And he'll stick with the man who displays it.

KEEP HIM INFORMED

Here again we overlap with follow through. For surely you'll win your customer's confidence when he knows that you'll feed him vital information in time for him to do something about it.

William Appleby of the National Adjustment Bureau has earned a reputation for reliability by leveling with his customers immediately if anything goes wrong. He cites a typical example.

"We ran into a five-week delay on one tough claim because all our men were tied up in a disaster area. Because I was frank with the customer and advised him we'd be late, he cooperated extremely well. He brought in an independent adjuster to get the case started, but with the understanding that we would take over when ready.

"Had I not kept him informed, he would probably have engaged the man to do the entire job, charging the difference to us. And he might well have started sending other claims out. This reputation for giving our clients the real score has gained us extra business over the years."

The Radiation Effect

Selling your personal reliability can also take the more positive form of keeping the client informed of various money making possibilities. In turn, the customer will often open the door to new prospecting leads.

It is fitting that we end this section with the case of a very successful investment salesman who has strengthened his relationships over the years by proving to be a reliable source of information on the overall market situation. If he can't call in person, he keeps his customers informed by phone.

One day he made a call on a major client to fill him in on an impending merger affecting one of the client's holdings. With the customer was an elderly woman who turned out to be an old friend of the family.

Turning to her, the client said: "Florence, I have never done business with anyone who has been so continually interested in what I am trying to do. I can really count on him to come by if he has something of interest to tell me."

About two weeks later, this woman phoned the salesman for an appointment. She had decided to change from her long-time counsel on investment matters, she explained, because "he calls only when he has something to sell."

The conclusion is clear. Your customers are the VIP's of your business life. Treat them in a way which shows that you consider them very important—and you won't have to worry about competitors muscling in.

C. HELP THEM KEEP YOU IN MIND

Every salesman tries to have his customers keep him in mind even though he may be out of sight. Those who succeed, generally follow three selling yourself rules:

1. Maintain contact . . . constructively.
2. Leave constructive personal reminders.
3. Remember the personal touch.

Let us discuss each of these in turn.

1. MAINTAIN CONTACT . . . CONSTRUCTIVELY

Earlier we discussed the constructive approaches designed to move the selling interview to a successful conclusion. Now we're talking about the in-between calls, those that let your customer know you're still alive and panting for more business.

Have a Reason for Calling

Too often such calls degenerate into little more than courtesy visits— or in Dick Borden's expressive phrase: "here-I-am-again" call. Seldom do they benefit the customer or result in new business.

"Dropping in simply to say 'hello', surely can't hurt," you may object.

The point is that it's rarely worth the effort, of itself. And it can breed resentment as a time waster.

One buyer sums the matter up this way. "Nothing irritates a businessman more than to have a salesman stop by to pass the time of day. Saying 'hello' or talking about the weather is *not* 'selling yourself.'

"To build a productive relationship you've got to drop in for a reason. The welcome mat is always out for the salesman who comes by with something helpful in mind."

Make It Useful . . .

Keeping in touch constructively does pose a problem for the intangibles salesman. For in most cases, his services or "products" do not suffer from wear and tear, or from obsolescence in the usual sense. In fact, in many intangibles fields such as insurance, you have an appreciation rather than depreciation, improvement instead of deterioration.

So it's hard to find a good reason for making frequent personal contact with the client.

But remember: to be helpful, the call need not be related to your service at all. Nor does it have to be in person—you can keep in touch just as easily and constructively by mail or phone.

Work out an organized program for this purpose. Build up a file of practical information for each client: take your visits and phone calls out of the here-I-am-again category by having something useful to offer each time.

. . . And Make It Different

Most salesmen follow one or more methods of maintaining contact. But when you do it thoughtfully, with a touch of imagination, the impact is all the greater. For example, when reading something which may be of interest to their customers and prospects, some salesmen will clip it, make copies and send them out.

One man makes the same act different by circling the item with thick black crayon, writing the customer's name alongside in red: "Pete: Thought you'd be interested." Then signs his name. That's all—but it stands out and it's remembered.

Clippings from technical bulletins, trade papers, Xeroxed pages from books are all grist to his mill.

Let Them Know How You're Doing

Nothing succeeds like success. This may be a bromide but it's nevertheless true.

One of the surest ways of selling yourself into continued business is to let your clients know when you've made a really good sale to a prominent concern or individual. A friend of mine sends out the following letter to all his current customers and centers of influence whenever he lands an order which will have considerable interest to his field.

It is quite informal, as you see, and easily adaptable to different situations.

> Dear John:
>
> You have always been very much interested in my progress and business, and your interest has been very much appreciated. I want you to know that I am anxious to continue to be worthy of it and am therefore taking this opportunity to tell you about my most recent client of considerable importance.
>
> Last week the Bosworth Company purchased from me a

group insurance and stock purchase plan for their employees. Both my company and I are very proud to add Bosworth to our customer list. It is a fine old company which has never stopped growing since it was first created. As you know, they are one of the leading manufacturers of dies for the automotive and farming industries.

May I take this opportunity to thank you again for all your helpfulness to me in the past, and I hope it will be my privilege to be of further service to you and to your friends.

Sincerely yours,

Landing a Big One

General insurance men dealing in fire and casualty insurance will often work for years to get a so-called "target-risk" away from a competitor. A man who convinces a major advertiser to move from one agency to another, will have previously made any number of constructive contacts.

Almost always, such sales turn on some extra step that sells the client on the salesman's ability to do a better job than the current supplier. And with both the old and the prospective supplier pouring it on, a final constructive touch can spell the difference.

Insurance man Harry Young, for example, had been working on an important corporate account for a long time, without success. He had wined and dined the Assistant Treasurer; had sent in a case of Scotch to the Treasurer the previous Christmas.

But the story remained the same. The firm believed its insurance was in good shape and no further coverage was necessary.

Finally, he made one truly constructive contact. With the help of his home office, Harry prepared an attractive brochure which showed in a series of case histories how much other firms had lost because of incomplete protection. Then it went on to illustrate the coverage designed for clients whose insurance needs had been analyzed by a meticulous survey.

The brochure concluded with a carefully detailed technical description of the work his agency would perform in making a survey for this firm.

Previously, the Treasurer had been friendly enough. But only now, impressed by this constructive effort, did he refer Harry's suggestions to the company's insurance committee.

Several months later, the committee agreed to the survey. When the eventual report recommended changes which added up to a considerable savings, Harry was authorized to take over the entire account.

2. LEAVE CONSTRUCTIVE REMINDERS

Most salesmen do leave or send reminders of one sort or another. The mails are clogged with calendars, for instance, come the year's end. And blotters with advertising on them clutter up many a desk.

Here again, your reminders will pay extra dividends when you work at making them different—and useful.

Calendars with a Twist

One successful salesman out west deals with oil companies. Every year, he sends his customers—and some prospects as well—two wall maps. Each has a calendar, but they also show clearly the current oil situation in the customer's area. Of course, they bear the salesman's name and carry an advertising plug.

These maps are so good that they have become almost essential to many of his clients. When a lease dealer comes into the buyer's office to discuss a possible lease, he is asked to pinpoint the area on the wall maps. The buyer can immediately tell if his firm would be interested or if further discussion would be waste of time.

Use Your Imagination

True, those maps are quite expensive. But a constructive reminder need not entail an appreciable outlay to solidify customer relations. All it takes is a knowledge of client needs wedded to a modicum of imagination.

In the previous chapter, for example, we saw how a simple chart outlining the various uses of a line of lubricants boosted one man from back-up position to favored supplier.

Another man has a wide collection of simple but practical reminders—ranging from technical bulletins to slide rules. "That way I can vary my reminders," he says, "leaving a different one on each visit."

You can best decide on the kind of reminder that will do the job for you.

3. REMEMBER THE PERSONAL TOUCH

Once you've laid the proper foundation, gained the client's confidence, and maintained constructive contact—you've crossed the biggest "selling yourself" hurdles. Beyond that, a genuine interest in your customer as a *person*, imparts a warmth which adds the overtones of friendship to what is essentially a business relationship.

Do It Naturally

As one representative points out, the best way to be friendly is *not* to pretend—but to take an active interest in the things that mean a lot to both of you.

As he writes: "How I do it depends on the customers. In some cases, I'll talk about his hobby with real enthusiasm because it's my hobby too. If it isn't, I don't get into it.

"Or I'll compare notes on his grandchildren and mine because we both get a kick out of our kids and their families."

Of course, there are no general rules everyone can follow in making friends and getting customers to like you. Some can pick up a tab and make it a gesture of friendship, rather than of business. The main thing is to do it in a natural way.

If you've got to force it, forget it, for the artificiality will seep through and the effect will be negative.

Be Different

Most salesmen do a good job on the personal side of customer relations. Yet here too, when you do it thoughtfully, spice your gesture with a touch of imagination, the impact is all the greater.

It Was Just the Book He Wanted

Here is a case which, appropriately enough, involved a sales training consultant. The idea can be applied to any business.

"I had a bank prospect for a program to help the officers sell their banking services more creatively. My prospect headed a department which was usually forward-looking and deeply involved in community affairs. I was exceptionally busy at the time and made just one call. And I knew that a competitor had made a number of calls, including a considerable amount of entertainment.

"Thinking about the problem of outdoing my competitor, I recalled an inspiring book I had read which seemed to me to underscore the forward-looking philosophy of my prospect. So I sent him a copy inscribing the fly leaf with the thought that here was a thinker who shared many of his ideas.

"Shortly after he started to read this book. He was so intrigued that he kept at it a good share of the night.

"Who was he thinking of? You guessed it. I got the business."

Yes, it pays to be different.

Flowers—or a Birthday Cake?

An insurance salesman had been planning to send flowers to a customer who was celebrating his twenty-fifth anniversary in business. However, when he envisioned the profusion of flowers that would be descending on the client's door, he had second thoughts about the matter.

In place of the flowers, he sent a big inscribed birthday cake. Everybody at the party tasted the cake, knew where it came from. When the story of the anniversary appeared in the local press, the cake and the donor were mentioned.

What happened to those who gave flowers? They each received an identical note of appreciation. But the next time our salesman called, the members of the firm thanked him profusely for his thoughtfulness.

Yet as that salesman told me later, the cake actually cost less than the flowers he had originally planned to order.

D. CULTIVATE NEW CONTACTS

It is almost impossible for an intangibles salesman to have too many contacts among the people who are prospects for his services. On the contrary: the great danger is that he will not have enough—that he will become too dependent on a small circle of friends or business associates.

To avoid this danger, you must sell yourself not only to existing customers but to as many contacts as possible who are potential buyers or who can open the door to potential business. You can join a trade association whose members use your services extensively; you can become active in community affairs.

Nor should you neglect such conventional methods as belonging to clubs or playing golf on a Sunday. It's easy enough to poke fun at "19th hole" shenanigans. Yet many a deal has been arranged or important leads picked up at the club bar.

The Introduction Did It

No one can tell in advance which contact will be the vital one in a given case. But the greater the number of people who are sold on you, the greater the possibility that one of them will prove to be just the man you need in a given case.

One brokerage man, for example, had been trying for a long time to get the account of a prospect who was a partner in a flourishing food distribution firm. One day the broker's queries disclosed that the man was trying to sell the prestige country club the broker belonged to.

Since he was on good terms with the steward, it was no trick to arrange for the food distributor to meet with the steward under highly favorable conditions.

Result?

The distributor got his account—and so did the broker.

In cultivating contacts, use the same principles employed in cultivating customers. Be helpful; win their confidence; be friendly—and keep in touch.

CAPSULE SUMMARY

How can you sell yourself effectively? By doing consistently what most of us do only to a degree.

This means in the first place following an organized program designed

to cultivate good customer relations. Such a program should include five
things in particular:

1. Make yourself the "buyer's friend" by taking pains to work
   out constructive ideas slanted at *his* problems.
2. Be reliable: make sure you follow through on every promise
   —and *never* oversell.
3. Help him keep you in mind with *constructive* contacts and
   reminders.
4. Don't forget the *personal touch*—but apply it sincerely and
   with flair.
5. *Sell yourself* continually to likely prospects or prospecting
   contacts.

12

How to Insure Your Future
as a Constructive Intangibles Salesman

If you follow through consistently, and sell yourself effectively, you'll get along nicely indeed: piling up a respectable sales record, drawing down a decent income. Most of us are satisfied if we can do just that, and rightly so.

But in every field of endeavor—in business, the arts, and the professions—you will always find the few who can never be satisfied with anything less than top level performance. It is from the ranks of these few that we get the "greats"—those whose performance puts them at the very top of their respective fields.

Those at the top conform to no simplistic formula. Yet for all their differences in style, in method and in personality, the selling greats—like outstanding performers in every field—do have one thing in common: those practices which help them stretch their abilities to the utmost.

They are strongly self-motivated: driven by their own inner desires. They never stop growing: never stop adding to their knowledge or command of technique. And when beset by the doldrums that inevitably plague us all, when everything turns sour, when making the rounds is a drag and productivity tails off—they know how to break through.

Luckily, this triple-pronged growth factor is an acquired ability. And as you learn how to motivate yourself, how to follow a self-development plan, and how to avoid going stale—you provide for yourself the finest "future insurance" possible in this uncertain world.

A. HOW TO MOTIVATE YOURSELF

Why does one man make it where another man fails? Osborne Elliot, one of the editors of *Fortune* addressed himself to that question as he contemplated the careers of the chief executives of some of the country's largest corporations for his book, *Men At The Top.*

On the surface, his subjects had little in common. One had won his college degree with honors, another had been a campus playboy, a third had dropped out of school when a good selling job had come his way. In temperament, they ranged the spectrum from outgoing geniality to self-centered intensity. And all had reached the top in different ways.

In sum, each was an individual sharply differentiated from any of the others. Then what quality did they share in common to explain their mutual success?

The more Elliott researched, interviewed and pondered, the clearer became the answer. For as far back as they could remember, he found, most men at the top knew exactly what they wanted. Always they had an eye on the top rung of their personal career ladders and headed toward it consciously.

Everything they did was colored by this long-range vision. And every success along the way merely whetted their desire to reach the top, as all eventually did.

THE POWER OF PERSONAL OBJECTIVES

"Compared to what we ought to be," said William James, America's great psychologist, "we are only half awake. The human individual possesses physical and mental resources of various sorts which he habitually fails to use."

Tapping those inner resources more fully is the key to success in any endeavor. In *On The Origin of Species,* Charles Darwin underlines the point. "Men differ less in the sum of their abilities than in the degree to which they use them."

What sets the superlative off from the mediocre is not how much you have but how much you use. And that, in turn, rests upon the strength of your inner drive. Or as Whitey Ford put it in an article on the ingredients of major league success: "First you've got to have desire."

Not that "can do" factors may safely be neglected. It is just that "will do" factors are somewhat more important because they bring into action more of those hidden resources which help the motivated man surpass himself. And of all the motivational forces which tug at our dormant powers, none even approaches the powerful impact of a man's own meaningful goals.

Putting It To the Test

In this connection, the general sales manager of a leading intangibles firm tells an interesting story. Having been impressed by a seminar on management-by-objectives (MBO), he decided to test the effect of goal-setting at the individual level. To this end, he picked two different territories, each fairly well matched in the abilities of its field managers and the productivity of its salesmen.

Company sales objectives were spelled out in detail for the four field managers involved. But from here on in matters diverged.

"Can you and your men together work out goals you will shoot for individually within the framework of the company objectives?" the sales manager asked the two "Group One" managers. After meeting with their crews, the two field supervisors reported on the goals their men had selected after heated discussion. Five things were included:

- managing time more fruitfully.
- cultivating 50% more prospects than were currently on their lists.
- selling a more rounded line.
- learning more about applications.
- increasing sales volume by 40% over the previous year.

At this point the top sales executive issued a directive to the "Group Two" managers and salesmen: saddling them with the same goals Group One had chosen for itself. A week later, when Group One *asked* if management could provide some training sessions on applications, Group Two was *told* that a training course had been scheduled which all must attend.

Six months later, a progress review disclosed some startling divergences between the two groups. Both had increased their output. But where Group One was running some 10% *above* its self-chosen goals, Group Two was about 20% *below* its imposed quotas.

"When we explained it was all an experiment," the general sales manager reports, "we got at the morale factors. Group Two supervisors and men felt they were 'being pushed around.' The Group One people welcomed it because 'it was what we asked for.'"

Winding up the story, the sales manager remarks: "We have since spread the idea to our entire sales force of having sales objectives set by those responsible for achieving them."

Make Them Your Own

As this story demonstrates, among other things, *you* should determine for yourself the directions your sales goals should take. They can focus on anything from time management to follow through: whatever areas of the selling process you want to strengthen.

Whatever objectives you choose, you can add to their inspirational power by adhering to four broad guidelines: Raise your sights. Make your goals measurable. Draw up follow through plans. Set up controls.

1. RAISE YOUR SIGHTS

That goals pave the way to success would need no further elaboration were it not for one inescapable fact. Everyone has aspirations, but few attain them.

Why the achievement gap? Mostly because we pitch our aim too low.

Take the aptly named "underachiever," the man who falls far short of his potential. Aspiring to little more than his weekly pay check, he adjusts to the level of the limited demands he makes on himself—his performance no longer keeps pace with his talents.

It's All In the Head

Let him once adopt an ambitious goal, however, and he begins to act in a new manner. Consider the saga of Frank Hollis, "a good man who was in a rut," as banker Roger Elwood puts it.

Hollis, mortgage officer in a suburban bank where Elwood was the manager, had for years been content with the business that found its way to his desk in the normal run of things. Apart from occasional literature rack concentration, he did little or nothing in the way of direct selling.

"Perhaps he'd still be in that rut if two things hadn't occurred," Elwood now says. "First, a savings and loan association opened a nearby office and began making heavy inroads in our mortgage business. Second, I read a management book which put a lot of stress on developing objectives.

"So I called Frank in and told him we had to do something about the S and L competition. 'What do you have in mind?' he asked.

" 'That's just the point,' I countered: 'you're our mortgage expert. Could you check over your records and project a healthy increase that you might be able to swing for the next year?'

"It worked like a shot of adrenalin. This was Tuesday afternoon. On Friday he was in my office with his figures: a projected increase of 28%. What's more, he put on my desk a complete officer call plan designed to get him and our other mortgage men into the community. I adopted it in toto, and put him in charge."

At year's end, an increase of 29% was recorded. Elwood congratulated the mortgage officer, remarking: 'I guess your ambitious objective really made you hustle.'

" 'You can say that again,' Hollis answered with a grin. 'But hustle wasn't the main reason we pulled ahead.' Pointing to his head, he said: 'It was all up here. With that big 28% nudging at me, I could no longer be satisfied with a 'good enough' day.

" 'I had to give one more hour to studying customer needs; figure out one new twist for an interview. Believe me, I'm going to start every year by putting down on paper the most ambitious goals I can set for myself.' "

Here we see the reason for the qualitative change in Hollis' actions. For the insistent pull of a challenging goal—one that demands every ounce of your capacity—forces you to reach inside yourself and enlist all the resources at your command.

2. MAKE THEM MEASURABLE

Objectives become most effective as motivators when they are measurable. That is, when every target is spelled out precisely, with figures and

time tables. As the sales manager of one of our largest insurance organizations reports. "Our records show that productivity goes up sharply when a man's efforts are directed toward specific, measurable goals."
Three things in particular account for this:
1. You make a deeper commitment to yourself.
2. The figures and deadline give you a continuing sense of urgency.
3. You get a built-in control.

Put a Number To It

The results of improved performance will generally show up in terms of more interviews per week, more sales per interviews, higher overall volume, more sales of specific services in your line, or some other quantitative aspect. It is these expected results which make it possible to state your goals in measurable terms.

Little more need be said beyond the doing of it. Translate each goal into specific quantities, either in absolute form: 25 or more new clients by the end of the year, or in percentages: a 30% increase over the previous year.

Put a Date To It . . .

Don't set goals on an open-ended basis. You can rarely gain the sense of driving urgency that propels you to the finish line, unless you have a deadline nagging at you.

But allow some leeway. *Not* by January one. Rather, by the first of January, give or take a week.

Should an exact date be impossible, give a definite time period: in four to six months, at the outside.

. . . And Break It into Chunks

Where goals require several months or more for completion, break them into smaller, intermediate steps. For a series of small successes imparts a feeling of progress and achievement, builds confidence, and expands mental horizons.

In brief, putting a number to it and a time makes your objectives more real, your plans more meaningful. It helps you pace yourself properly, helps you break down your ultimate goal into easy stages.

3. PLAN FOR IT

Your plans will vary with your goals. However, one fairly safe conclusion can be drawn: Your goals may turn out to be little more than wishful thinking unless you do plan for them, one way or another.

Not that such plans need be elaborate. One mutual funds salesman, for example, set as one of his goals a 25% increase in the number of referrals from existing customers.

His plan? Methodically, he phoned every client, frankly explained why he was calling and asked for names of friends and relatives "who would benefit from selective mutual funds investment." He wound up with more than double the percentage increase he had aimed for.

4. SET UP CONTROLS

With your figures, deadlines, and plans, you have supplied your own built-in controls. But you as self-manager must activate the machinery.

Obviously, you can't wait until time has run out before checking on your progress. Schedule a full-scale review for yourself at weekly, monthly, or quarterly intervals, depending upon the given circumstances.

That way, you're always on top of the ball. And you can follow through immediately, wherever corrective action should be required.

One man who sells a line of intangible "products" meets his self-imposed quotas simply by checking on his results as he goes along.

"I find it a good idea," he says, "not only to establish quotas by numbers, but also by profit items. That is, items that generally carry a larger margin. I keep an account of my sales in these high margin services— posting it weekly on top of my desk so that I can see where I am lagging behind.

"In addition to this, about every two months I go through each customer's invoices for a rundown on the various items he buys. This tells me what percentage of his 'profit business' I am getting and on what items I must concentrate in order to increase my profit with that account."

However you do it, some method of control will reinforce the effect of self-motivating objectives.

B. FOLLOW A SELF-DEVELOPMENT PLAN

If self-motivation supplies the initial power, self-development beefs it up in supercharger fashion whenever the situation requires. A self-development plan should encompass three broad areas of practical knowledge:

1. Become a walking encyclopedia: of product knowledge, of customer knowledge, of competitor knowledge, of ideas and applications.

2. Learn to use sales tools effectively.

3. Broaden your horizons beyond the limits of business and selling.

1. BECOME A WALKING ENCYCLOPEDIA

Most men agree that a good working knowledge of their own services, of competitor offerings, and customer needs will normally be a major factor in successful selling. For the most part, however, they rest content with the information provided by their home offices and with what comes their way in the course of experience.

But to insure your future: to pull ahead of the crowd—and stay ahead, you must go well beyond this. You must *work* at it so consistently and so systematically that you become a walking encyclopedia of practical knowledge.

Consider such fields as office systems, group insurance, and the sale of computer services. Because of the special training their companies provide, the average salesmen in those areas do a brisk, competent job. But the men who shoot to the top are those who become *the recognized authorities* in their respective fields. Prospects seek out such men because of their constructive ideas and knowledge of applications.

For example, a man well versed in the benefits to be gained from insuring the lives of employees, their health, and the health of their families can generally make a go of it in group insurance. But if he wants to be a top producer now and in the foreseeable future, he must pay the price in time and effort of becoming a specialist in depth. Among other things, this means going beyond the mechanisms and benefits of group coverage to an intensive study of salary and wage scales, health and accident hazards, and competitive offerings.

Attitudes Come First

To sell intangibles at all, let alone to do well enough to earn a decent living, you've got to start with a good understanding of your service, your customer and your competition. The real problem is complacency, the feeling that we already know all we need to know about what we sell.

Actually, the one lesson I have learned in a lifetime of selling intangibles is the need for constant growth: for learning more and more about my business and about the problems of present and potential clients.

I can well remember a purchasing agent who shamed me by his superior knowledge of what I thought was my special province When he saw how embarrassed I was about my comparative ignorance, he smiled and said: "Don't worry about it. I was in your business 25 years before becoming a purchasing agent."

But then he added by way of friendly advice: "If you want to stay ahead in this game, you've always got to keep one thing firmly in mind—that you can never know enough; can never stop learning."

Develop Your Plan . . . and Work It

Given the right frame of mind, half the battle is won. To complete the job you've got to work out a plan of study—then follow through religiously.

Naturally, the details will vary with your business. But the broad outlines of a self-development plan will generally include the following.

Develop an inquiring eye. Never let a day go by without trying to learn something new. When you see something that might be of value to your customers or help you in a presentation, turn an inquiring eye on it. Ask what, why and how: and don't be satisfied until you've got it down pat—perhaps in your head, perhaps in your personal "idea book."

Get in and watch. At intervals, ask your prospects and customers to let you explore their business or personal situations first hand. They will be happy to see that you take an active interest in their needs. You will bolster your knowledge.

Exchange ideas and information. No one person can possibly know the answers to every question that might arise in your line of business. But you can find the answers you need by tapping the accumulated knowledge of the hundreds of salesmen, buyers, businessmen, and executives you meet and deal with. You can do it at sales meetings, in your hotel of a night, at business conventions, or trade association meetings. Just engage regularly in a reciprocal exchange of ideas and information and the chinks in your information gap will slowly be filled in.

Know your sources. "Years ago when I was majoring in science," one salesman writes, "I found it impossible to commit to memory all the facts and formulae I needed. But learning where to look for them was easy.

"The same is true in selling. Gaining an intimate knowledge of every aspect of our services or customer needs is difficult, if not impossible. Knowing where to find and how to use reference material is simple enough. And it's all we need to know in most cases when tackling customer or selling problems."

Know your competition. Several years ago, I worked with a man who had been a freight solicitor for a major western railroad for a number of years. He became sufficiently well known among influential shippers to open an office as a shipping consultant for all types of freight transport services.

This man acquired his clientele largely because his extensive knowledge enabled him to render service far beyond "the call of duty." Because he made a point of knowing the schedules of every competitor, for example, he would arrange customer shipments via other carriers when his own railroad could not meet the client's immediate needs.

Follow a Reading Plan

In most fields you will find a vast reservoir of practical knowledge in books, pamphlets, and trade journals. Such knowledge, however, is of value to the individual salesman only to the extent that he dips into and uses it.

But no matter how much time we squeeze out for it, there's always far more to read than any one of us can digest.

An impasse? Not quite. For most of us have the same problem with prospects and customers. We always have more than we can possibly reach effectively.

What do we do in that case?

We use some sort of cream-separating device, we grade our prospects and concentrate on the best.

You can plan your reading on an equally selective basis. You might concentrate, for example, on literature that helps you prepare for specific accounts or that moves you toward some future goal.

One man grades his reading materials as must read, read if possible, and throw out. Every morning he allots 30 minutes for his "must" list. That way, he never lets it get out of hand.

At odd moments of the day, he wades through a fair amount of the "read if possible" pile. If it starts stacking up, he switches it over to the discard pile.

This rationalized reading plan keeps him one jump ahead in a highly competitive field. As he puts it: "I've compiled a wealth of information most of my competitors don't even know exists."

Copy, File and Index

One salesman firms up his "future insurance" reading by condensing every important bit into a series of "information notebooks." He clips, copies and files items of special interest to specific customers. Carefully indexed under descriptive headings, his personal information file has helped him keep a high percentage of customers in a field where current suppliers can be squeezed out overnight.

Make It a Habit

Much of the above has been elaborated upon in Chapter 4. Here, just two more things need be said of your "walking encyclopedia" plan.

First, the plan must be *yours:* must fit *your* needs, *your* business, *your* temperament.

Second, and most important, make it a habit. No matter how much or how little time you allocate to it—let nothing interfere with your scheduled self-development activities.

2. LEARN TO USE SALES TOOLS EFFECTIVELY

Do you get your interviews off to a good start by paving the way with a pre-approach telephone call? And do you use the telephone often enough as an aid to building repeat sales?

When you make your presentations, do you take advantage of the interviewing support provided by modern sales tools? Do you walk into the interview bolstered by a well-designed sales portfolio, comparison chart, or other sales aid that lets your prospect look as well as listen?

If your answer to such questions is "no," then you are offering your competition a decided advantage. Your services may be as good as theirs; your prices may match. But you will still lose otherwise obtainable business to competitors who outdo you in the creative use of good selling tools.

Most salesmen do use various sales tools to greater or lesser degree. But to get your share—and more—of the available market, consider how you can more effectively apply the two aids most useful in selling intangibles: the telephone and the visual.

How To Improve Your Telephone Technique

The do's and dont's of good telephone selling have been scattered through various chapters of this book. Basically, these boil down to one phrase: be prepared.

When you organize your desk: when you keep benefit briefs, applications information and customer files close to hand—you've taken your first long step toward better telephone selling. When you're prepared to be constructive before you dial, your chances of a warm response have been further enhanced.

And finally, when you're calling to arrange an interview, close a sale or follow through on one, you'll step up your "sell appeal" to the utmost by building a pleasant but forceful telephone personality.

Telephone "Sell Appeal"

In face-to-face selling, you can appeal to all five senses. Your prospect can see a sample, feel it, smell it. He can taste the drink you may be buying or the cigarette you offer him. He can respond to the smile on your face and to your gestures, as well as to the sound of your voice.

On the phone, you must depend on voice alone. Despite this great limitation, many telephone salesmen who seldom see their customers build relationships that are almost as cordial as those developed by outside salesmen. Somehow, they manage to transform themselves from disembodied voices to distinctive personalities.

How do they do it?

By projecting warmth, sincerity, forcefulness and enthusiasm over the telephone wire. For with careful attention to certain well-established techniques, each of these qualities can be reflected at the other end.

1. Visualize Your Prospect

What accounts for so much telephone detachment? We forget there's a person, a human being attached to the voice we're listening and talking to. Visualize a man at the other end: his face, his hands, his gestures—and your natural warmth will assert itself.

"I CLOSE MY EYES"

Some years ago, the Classified Advertising Department of a Los Angeles newspaper awarded prizes each quarter to the telephone salesmen who persuaded more people to place their ads on 7-time or 30-time contracts. Persistent winner Dorothy Handelman explains how she did it.

"Always I close my eyes while talking on the phone. Instead of looking at the mouthpiece, I visualize my customer mentally, sitting in a chair or at a desk, worried about personal or business problems, needing my help. I see him so clearly he becomes real to me. And I give him all my attention, focus my mind entirely on what he is saying."

Visualize your prospect and speak to him as though he were seated directly across the desk. For one thing, this will make you react to him warmly as a person, not just a voice. For another, visualizing him will help you speak in a more natural, more pleasing voice. Many of us unconsciously raise our voices on the phone as though to bridge the physical distance that separates us from our listeners.

2. Say It With a Smile

It's literally true. Smile when you talk and your smile will shine through.

But it must be genuine. Some salesmen who do a lot of telephone selling place a mirror where they can see their smiles reflected. The artificiality of this device will manifest itself on the wire just as surely as the painted smile of the professional glad-hander betrays insincerity in face-to-face contacts.

Your best bet? Visualize your prospect, as indicated above. Your voice will then convey the true warmth of a person-to-person smile.

3. Say It Slowly and Clearly: Sounding Every Letter in Every Word

You can hardly project sincerity, enthusiasm, or force when the person you're talking to must strain to understand you. Nor can you hold his attention overlong.

Because you appeal only to the sense of hearing, you must speak distinctly—sometimes more slowly than face-to-face. Otherwise, as every study indicates, many words and phrases just don't come through.

"Granted," you might say. "Careful diction makes for pleasanter telephone conversation. But what has this to do with selling?"

Quite a lot. Some insurance companies, for instance, prepare scripts which telephone sales representatives use to make appointments for outside salesmen. Several companies have retained speech specialists to help boost the percentage of appointments chalked up.

When trained to sound every letter in every word, these telephone salesmen *stepped up the number of appointments* by 25–40% on the average.

Everything else remained the same: same message, same territories, same salesmen. The only thing that changed was the voice. Now it was careful, precise, more colorful.

By sounding every letter, each salesman found he could more easily vary pitch, volume and speed of delivery. This variety of expression lent more color to his voice, added a new dimension to his telephone personality: one that paid off in this case with more appointments.

MAKE IT A HABIT

To acquire the habit of sounding every letter or syllable, practice it at every opportunity. Many salesmen make time for this when driving to their interviews and when heading for home or hotel in the evening.

When you are alone, try speaking out loud to yourself—carefully sounding every letter and syllable. And talk in a whisper, but as though you wanted someone 50 feet away to hear every word clearly. The moment you do this both your lips and larynx will come more fully into play.

Then, with your lips still working in the same manner, switch back from a whisper to your natural voice. Immediately, you will recognize the gain in range, in resonance and in force.

Work at it consciously and regularly. Sooner or later, this clearer, more forceful manner of speaking will become an integral part of your telephone personality.

Your face-to-face personality will benefit equally. Perhaps even more so, for you will find that those "er's" and "ah's" so common to the speech of most people, will tend to disappear.

4. Keep Your Sentences Short

Short sentences also help your prospects take in the full meaning of what you are saying. But there's more to it than that.

On the phone, more than in face-to-face selling, people resent listening to monologues. So keep your sentences short and pepper them with questions aimed at eliciting more than just "yes" or "no" responses. For as you provoke two-way discussion, you add another plus to the many factors which can eventually make or break a sale.

Visual Aids

Visual aids of various kinds make excellent tools for handling a variety of recurring situations. One type of selling situation which virtually cries for visual help occurs in busy offices or homes where the salesman must contend with constant interference. And as the thread of his story is lost, so is the sale.

Visuals help your story hang together in the first instance. Equally, you can more easily pick up and go again after an interruption, with little or no loss of cumulative force.

In this section, we consider the effective use of the two most powerful visual aids: the normal visual presentation and the comparison chart.

1. THE VISUAL PRESENTATION

As the story goes, Harold Ickes once raced through the Washington railroad terminal and leaped into a waiting taxi. The startled driver immediately shifted into gear and away they tore at high speed.

"Where are you going?" cried Ickes.

"I don't know," yelled the cabbie, "but I see you're in an awful hurry."

Too many salesmen have temperaments like that cabbie's. Sanguine and impressionable, they gallop off in any direction their prospects lead. With no orderly sequence of ideas to carry the prospect's mind from his interests to an appreciation of their services, they get too few signatures on their order blanks.

Buyers Prefer Visuals

In moving a prospect's mind from where it is to where you want it to be, a well-planned visual presentation does a neat job of cerebral transportation. Indeed, it tells its story so easily, so vividly and in so little time—that most buyers prefer to be sold that way.

As a study by *Purchasing* magazine confirms, more than 85% of all buyers find visuals more interesting and helpful than conventional interviews, and prefer to see the salesmen who use them. More to the point, *they buy more from them.*

Consider but one case of many which bears this out in practice. Johnson and Johnson prepared a visual for calls on retail druggists who did not stock the company's extensive line of surgical dressings. As reported to the Sales Executives Club of New York, there was not a single turndown in 22 consecutive exposures to prospects who had been saying "no" to the same salesmen for one to ten years past.

A Paradox

Here we enter the realm of paradox. Salesmen who have used visuals agree they can boost volume and earnings. Yet most of these same men who have experienced the selling power packed into a well-designed visual, shy away from them.

Why this paradoxical reaction?

Because the good salesman sees the visual as a canned talk that degrades his skills and reduces his role to that of an automaton, rigid and impervious to prospect and customer differences. To some extent, that fear is well founded. Yet properly used, negative factors can be minimized, positive factors magnified.

Whether you design your own or use a home-office mass produced portfolio, the following guide lines will help you make the most of it.

Design Your Own

Salesmen who fear the visual yet do recognize its value, rarely think of preparing their own. Why not?

Possibly because the seeming complexity of the professionally designed visual presentation scares them off. Actually, when you use photos with hand-blocked captions, testimonials, and customer letters to tie together the different parts of your story in such a way that you lead the prospect from one point to the next in a logical progression to your close—then you have made a visual presentation: whether or not you call it by that name.

Looked at in that fashion, salesmen use the selling power of a visual more often than they may realize. One man, for instance, secured an important account with the help of a home-made visual—though he didn't call it that. As far as he was concerned, he was just using a loose-leaf binder to hold all the evidence that proved what his firm could do and had done for others.

Two spreads were devoted to invoices, showing the wide variety of services this firm could offer. Other spreads had copies of direct mail promotions which demonstrated the firm's willingness to follow through in every way needed to guarantee customer satisfaction.

To underline the point, another spread had photos showing an adjuster in action. These pictures and the appended descriptive captions enabled the salesman to expand upon each point in his sales message. Finally, a spread which featured copies of customer correspondence indicated that the firm could handle complaints promptly and equitably.

In presenting his case, this salesman used the portfolio to introduce each point in turn—expanding upon it or not as prospect reaction dictated. As a result, he increased his sales to calls ratio by more than 30%.

Make It Fit the Job

A good visual begins with a realistic concept about the job to be done and the share of the load to be carried by the visual and by you. In designing (or applying) it, ask yourself these five questions:

1. What are the key points of your proposition, in general?
2. What are the key points for this prospect?
3. What are the conditions under which the presentation will be made?
4. Who is to be influenced?
5. What actions are desired?

Incorporate Tested Selling Principles

Begin with a door-opening promise. Loosen up the prospect with questions slanted at his needs. Sell the benefits—wrapping up each point carefully. Make room for objections. And close actively.

Make It Easy to Follow and Understand

This, perhaps, is the central rule for preparing—and using—an effective visual presentation: Cover one big idea at a time. How do you do it?
1. Put only one basic idea on a spread.
2. Hammer each one home with a wrap-up query before proceeding to the next spread.
3. Arrange each spread in a logical sequence with one buy point inevitably leading to the next. By placing the material to clinch each idea where it will do the most good, you accent the positive at the right psychological moment.

Let Yourself Star

Because of its step-by-step procedure, a well-designed visual gives you a planned sequence of selling points, effectively arranged, cogently phrased and dramatically illustrated. But *don't* let the visual star. *Don't* try to pack in the whole story, complete to the last detail. And *don't* read it directly: your prospect went to school, too!

Do use each spread with its single big idea as a jumping off point—with *you* filling in the details, asking and answering questions.

Keep It Flexible

Even with recurring situations, you will rarely if ever face two interviewing situations which are exactly alike. Each prospect's needs and problems vary in full or in detail from the next man's.

Home-made or home-office-designed, personalize your visual for each prospect or customer. One way, for example, is to devote some pages to glassine envelopes whose contents—photographs, sketches, testimonials, etc.—can be altered at will, depending on the circumstances of a given interview.

For flexibility, nothing beats an ordinary 8½×11 loose-leaf binder. You can easily tailor the story for different prospects by adding or subtracting pages. Should the need arise, you can change the sequence. And you can still retain the benefit of the glassine-envelope pages described above.

One salesman dissipated the effect of a beautifully made visual by covering the entire ground on every call. When he recognized that all he really wanted was a graphic way of telling the one part of his story a prospect wanted to hear, he asked the home office to switch from an easel form to loose-leaf. Armed with this more flexible sales tool, he went back and sold more than half of the prospects who had originally turned him down.

Follow these guidelines when designing or using your sales portfolio. You will thereby gain a most valuable and welcome kind of selling support.

2. THE COMPARISON CHART

Simple to construct, easy to adapt to different prospects, the comparison chart makes a powerful selling tool in the hands of a skillful intangibles salesman. Whether on the personal side or in business, most prospects will want to weigh the merits of competing offerings. So why not make it easy for them—while holding the reins in your own hands—by preparing a visual comparison?

Surely, if comparisons are important to the buyer, then helping him make comparisons must give a competitive advantage to the accommodating salesman. Robert Todt, who heads a firm providing an industrial cleaning and maintenance service, can testify to the truth of this.

"Because this is a highly competitive field," Todt observes, "most prospects hesitate to buy without a complete picture of comparative prices and quality. Besides, in some cases our competitors underbid us; unless we can justify our bid, there's no hope of a sale.

"To demonstrate the economics of superior service, we arm our men with a detailed, two-part comparison chart. The first table graphically depicts comparative prices and quality of the detergents, spray equipment and other materials used by our firm and our four major competitors.

"The second table gives a clear picture, item for item, of the longer life and fewer maintenance renewals characteristic of our line. This dramatizes the superior performance that justifies our price differentials.

"Few of our prospects have the time to prepare such an objective comparison themselves. This information represents a real service to them—and they reciprocate with orders. Since our men started using these charts extensively, many sales have been closed without our competition even having a chance to bid."

"Do you need professional help in preparing them?" Todt was asked.

"Only if we want some fancy art work. We prepare our own, together with our salesmen.

"You've just got to be sure you present your competitor's case fairly. Once your prospect doubts the honesty or accuracy of your presentation, you're dead."

By using a comparison chart, you've got five things going for you

1. When you compare, you do something prospects understand, accept and appreciate.

2. Direct comparisons with your competitors dramatize your confidence in your plan.

3. They provide strong, supportive proof for the benefits you claim for your service.

4. Comparisons offer the prospect a reasoned choice: with you there to see that your service gets the best of it.

5. Comparisons suggest *action:* buy this, not that.

Broaden Your Horizons

Many presidents of major companies have come up through the line of sales, having started as salesmen at the lowest level. Chief among the reasons for their success is the fact that over the years these men acquired a broad knowledge of their businesses by doing the very things we have been talking about in the preceding sections of this chapter—*plus* a generous measure of extra-curricular activities which gave them the breadth and stature their present positions require.

It has been my privilege to know several of these men both when they were on their way up and after they had arrived. All of them gave and still give special attention to three aspects of self-development aimed at broadening their horizons.

1. They keep making new contacts *outside* their fields of work.

2. They keep abreast of current events and current thought.

3. They enjoy and participate in diversions which let their mental and physical energies spill over into areas completely unrelated to business.

One of my best and must successful "presidential" friends calls this type of activity "Recharging the batteries with fresh power." Another calls it "Job Therapy."

A Balanced Program

Although they've reached the top, these men never stop looking to the future. All of them read widely. Many keep right on with some kind of formal education, whether through company-sponsored training programs or via some type of correspondence courses. Two of them attend the summer schools run by the Harvard Business School and the Bankers' School of Rutgers.

Nor do they neglect two other factors conducive to mental, physical and emotional balance. Each of these men takes up some physical activity from golf, tennis, or gardening to hiking, jogging, and cycling. And each devotes a fair amount of time to family and social affairs.

You can insure your own future in exactly the same way. By remembering that you're a man as well as a salesman, by engaging in outside activities which keep you mentally and physically alert, you too will retain your zest for living, enlarge your imagination, and keep from growing stale.

And the funny thing is, that in broadening your horizon as a whole man, you will directly enhance your work as a salesman. For when you read such publications as *New Yorker, The Saturday Review, Newsweek, Business Week, Fortune* and the *Sunday New York Times;* when you can intelligently discuss domestic politics, social problems ranging from black power to the generation gap, international affairs, and the arts—you can sell yourself to an ever-widening circle of prospects and customers.

Besides, such reading and discussion keeps your "imagination quotient" high: makes you more likely to get in front and stay in front with constructive ideas.

C. HOW TO BREAK THROUGH THE DOLDRUMS

Practically everything in this book has been designed as an antidote for dry runs or going stale. Still, in a lifetime of selling, you're bound to hit the dog days.

You just don't feel like selling. Your spirits droop, your feet drag, your presentations limp.

Or you're trying as hard as ever, but suddenly nothing works, you can't make a sale. Soon you're forcing the pace, but your anxiety gets in the way.

What to do?

In most cases, a change of pace is clearly indicated. This can take two forms.

On the business side, make something happen. On the personal side, change your rhythms.

Let's see what this means in practice.

1. MAKE SOMETHING HAPPEN

Most of us accept the need for an occasional change of pace in our personal lives. Yet we arely carry over this instinctive wisdom to the business world.

When floundering around in a rut, we force ourselves through the motions of a routine that has temporarily turned sour or totally unproductive. Why not give yourself a lift instead with the exhilarating freedom of a break in schedule? Why not make something unexpected happen by stepping outside the planned activities of the day or week?

One Caution

Here a caution is in order. *Don't* try to force the pace where a deal is in the works. Your sense of desperation will more likely push you out of the picture than break you through.

You Can Do It Simply

Your breakthrough might be aimed, for example, at some old but high potential prospect who may never have given you business. Or you might cast a thoughtful eye on some customer who has been inactive of late.

For my own part, when sales suddenly dry up I often break my routine in a simple enough manner. I merely look through my files and start phoning some old contacts I've neglected for a long time.

The results can at times be truly uncanny. It's as though some of these people were sitting there, waiting for my call.

Actually, there's nothing mysterious about it. After all, you're a salesman. On your previous contacts you probably did a workmanlike missionary job. Even though it didn't take at the time, it keeps working on the prospect just below the level of consciousness.

Comes the unexpected phone call and you spark him into the positive action that winds up in an order—and snaps you out of the doldrums.

You Can Aim at a Big One

Of course, this simple maneuver won't always work. In that case, start making things happen on a somewhat grander scale.

You might, for example, galvanize your thinking by aiming at a bigger sale than you ordinarily might. Consider the case of Phil Storrs. As he tells it, he landed a sale he would never have tried for had he not been in the middle of a long-standing drought.

Phil operates out of Springfield for Consolidated Finance, a local business-financing organization. For some time, he recalls, stubborn adherence to his scheduled round of calls had done little more than weaken his morale. One morning, after a discussion with his boss, Phil decided to drop everything for a while and make a pitch for the account of Acme Development, a state-wide realty corporation with home offices in Central City.

"We didn't really expect to get anywhere with them; but we both agreed that I needed a break in routine. We knew that Acme was considering construction of a mammoth shopping center just outside of Springfield. But we also knew that First National of Central City usually supplied all their financial needs.

"Normally, I would have sounded out the Acme management before committing myself to any preliminary investigation. But I wanted to shake myself up mentally by operating outside routine.

"Besides, this was a big sale against big competition. *I had to make things happen* if I were to have any chance at all.

"For both these reasons, I worked on this as though I had a contract or a strong expression of interest at the very least. When I was ready, I arranged an appointment and drove out to Central City for a conference with Acme Treasurer Silas Adamson.

"Adamson listened to me politely. Then he said: 'Sorry, Mr. Storrs, but First National takes care of all our needs—and they've been most helpful to us in our business transactions here.'

"Of course. First National serves you better than we can here because it knows Central City so well."

(This was a neat touch, opening the way for stressing Consolidated's ability to do a job on its own home grounds).

"But that's exactly the point," Phil continued. "On your local deals a home-town outfit is usually your best bet.

"Frankly, Mr. Adamson, I know you're about ready to move on that shopping center. But I've been thinking about your other property investments in Springfield. Sometimes you've taken a loss there, haven't you?"

"True."

"That's where we can help. Our realty specialists can tell you many things you may want to know about property in our city, what it's worth, the income it pays, and whether property values in that neighborhood are moving up or down."

Here Mr. Adamson broke in. "Granting a local tie makes sense, how do we know you could do a job for us in the pending deal?"

At that point Phil relaxed. For his opening shot, based on his study of Acme's previous investments in Springfield, had been accepted in principle. It remained only to sell his firm's ability to help in the current situation. And there his preliminary investigation had put him in the driver's seat.

By the time he finished laying on the line all the hard facts he had gathered, Adamson was ready to refer the proposal to the firm's finance committee. Eventually, the big sale was made.

But for Phil the moral goes deeper. "Sure, I was happy to make the sale and the big commission that went with it. However, even if it hadn't gone through, the thought and effort I put into it would have shaken me out of my slump. Before the sale was closed, I found myself ready to go back to my regular schedule with all the pep I used to have. There's no better way to get out of a rut than to do something different."

2. CHANGE YOUR PERSONAL RHYTHMS

Sometimes, when your work goes stale, nothing you do on the job will snap you out of it. Usually, this signals the fact that your personal life has gone out of whack; your nose has been on the grindstone far too long.

So shake up your personal life. Do something you haven't done for a long time. Something you enjoy, but "couldn't make the time for."

If your single, go out on the town for a couple of nights. If you're married, buy your wife some French perfume or take her and the kids out for a show and dinner. Their enjoyment at this break in routine will communicate itself to you.

If this doesn't work, take a couple of days off. Often, that's all that's needed. Go fishing, take in a ball game, get in a round of golf, take the kids camping, read a good book.

If this doesn't get you back raring to go, you'd better see a doctor.

Incidentally, even when you're not stuck in the doldrums, an occasional change of personal rhythms is a good form of "future insurance." It keeps you mentally and physically alert—ready to snap up every opportunity that comes your way.

CAPSULE SUMMARY

Future insurance symbolizes the steps you take to keep your sales sold in the foreseeable and unforeseeable future and to help you keep moving to the top of your personal career ladder.

This means in the first place that you motivate yourself with a succession of ambitious objectives. As soon as you achieve one, you set your sights on and plan for another.

It means that you never stop growing: That you plan and follow through on a never-ending series of development plans, plans to make you a walking encyclopedia of practical knowledge, a skilled user of modern sales tools, a rounded individual conversant with politics, social problems, and the arts.

It means, finally, preparing yourself for the inevitable dog days with a tested bag of unscheduled, self-galvanizing activities. By providing the change of pace we all require at times, such activities will snap you out of the doldrums before anxiety and desperation dig you in deeper.

Index